Wrecks & Reefs

OF SOUTHEAST SCOTLAND

MIKE CLARK

Whittles Publishing

Published by
Whittles Publishing,
Dunbeath,
Caithness KW6 6EG,
Scotland, UK

www.whittlespublishing.com

© 2010 Mike Clark
ISBN 978-184995-010-7

Printed by Bell & Bain Ltd., Glasgow

CONTENTS

Preface   v
Acknowledgements   vi
Introduction   vii
    How to use this guide   vii
    How to get there   vii
    Where to stay   viii
    Tides   viii
    Diving Qualifications Explained   ix
    The Diver's Code of Conduct   x

BURNTISLAND   1

NORTH BERWICK   18

ISLE OF MAY   39

DUNBAR   56

ST ABBS   79

EYEMOUTH   134

Dive Centres   172
Sources and further reading   179

SOUTH EAST SCOTLAND

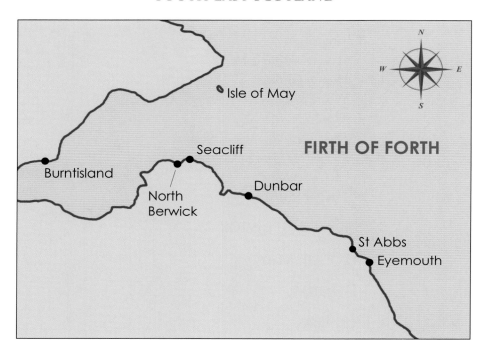

Isle of May

FIRTH OF FORTH

Seacliff

Burntisland

North
Berwick

Dunbar

St Abbs

Eyemouth

PREFACE

Edinburgh's port of Leith, which lies on the south side of the Firth of Forth, has served since medieval times as a large and important shelter for shipping. Originally, when tourists had yet to discover the delights of Scotland's east coast, it was a base for warships and for trading vessels loaded with wine and other produce for import and export around Europe, while today Leith is an important port of call for cruise ships

Further west, on the north side of the river and just west of the Forth Bridge, lies Rosyth Dockyard, where the Royal Navy maintained a strong presence through both world wars. Today the dockyard is used for the refitting of naval ships and serves as a passenger terminal for ferry services to Europe.

So even this, just the inner part of the Firth of Forth, has historically been home to two major destination points for vessels. This busy waterway has seen many ships caught up in storms, failing to avoid collisions or falling victim to raiding U-boats or aircraft in wartime. From Leith Docks, the river opens up to form a huge estuary filled with volcanic islands and submerged pinnacles, blasted by fierce tidal streams. It is also the final resting place of hundreds of ships, many of which are of enormous historical importance.

This book has been written because there is, for the diver, so much to explore, most of it unknown to the vast majority of people: a wrecked aircraft carrier, a German light cruiser which, unlike the ones in Scapa Flow, did see action at the battle of Jutland, aircraft and even steam-powered submarines. Fantastic wrecks which, incredibly, have barely been dived. Unlike the Clyde wrecks on the west coast of Scotland, or the wrecks in the English Channel that have been well dived and documented, the wrecks of the Firth of Forth rarely get a mention, even though many lie within a twenty-mile radius of Edinburgh. The area's impressive scenic diving is also often overlooked.

This divers' guide begins at the famous Forth Bridge and travels east, exploring the wrecks and reefs of the Firth of Forth and the southeast of Scotland, passing through the important diving areas of Burntisland, North Berwick, Dunbar, St Abbs and Eyemouth, examining all the exciting newly-discovered dive sites along the way and suggesting how best to dive them. Although dive sites do exist further upstream, poor visibility hinders diving activities there. I have dived all the sites and wrecks within this guide and, as an underwater photographer, have done my best to capture images that convey to the reader the special identity of the individual east coast wrecks and reefs.

Mike Clark

ACKNOWLEDGEMENTS

I first dived in 1986 at Pettico Wick and this book is the culmination of 25 years experience of diving in the Firth of Forth. Why have I dived so long? Well it's down to the excitement I still get from being underwater but also from the good people I have met who have helped me.

I would like to thank my parents, Maureen and Robert. They helped make my dream come true on my 21ˢᵗ birthday by enabling me to purchase a Birchley Products housing for my Practica BC3 camera. This started me on my career in underwater photography. Also my wife Lynn and children Jamie and Emma who have put up with my diving absences, especially over the last 6 months when I have undertaken the preparation of this book. Thanks also Bill and Greta for all their help and support.

I learnt to dive in the club era and there are many people to thank for that: Graeme Tough, Charlie Murnin from Telford Branch and Ian Morrison from Divetech; Dougie McEwan of the Edinburgh Diving Centre; also Alex Struthers for all the good dives and the work done on the Aquanaut and to Geoffrey Scott, Crawford Bailie and Martin Sinclair. I am grateful to the British Sub Aqua Club for permission to reproduce their code of conduct and diving qualifications.

Lately I have been learning Technical Diving Skills to safely explore the deeper wrecks of the Firth of Forth and thanks goes to Gordon Mackay of GM Diving and Stevie Gibson of TT Diving both of whom have been of great assistance. Relationships with dive boat skippers are important to me and I must thank Peter Gibson for helping me out with a few projects over the years and Mark Blyth for supplying the GPS coordinates for the sites around Burntisland. Lastly and certainly not least I would like to thank Jim and Iain Easingwood of Marine Quest who have been so enthusiastic and found so many new dive sites and for supplying all the remaining GPS coordinates in this book. There are too many people to mention in this limited space, but to all the divers and underwater photographers who I have chin wagged with over the years, shared advice and had a good laugh – all the very best and hopefully see you soon.

INTRODUCTION

HOW TO USE THIS GUIDE

This guide has been created to flow, like the Firth of Forth, from west to east. It starts at the famous Forth Bridge and works ever further south and east as the Forth enters the North Sea, until it reaches the border with England. I have grouped the dive sites around nearby towns which have a diving operation and which would make the best base from which to explore a particular area. The five sections covered by this book are Burntisland, North Berwick (including the Isle of May), Dunbar, St Abbs and Eyemouth. I have included maps to assist with the location of shore diving sites and have also included the recommended level of diving experience required to dive each site. For the boat dives I have, where available, provided GPS coordinates, kindly supplied by Marine Quest for all sites apart from the Burntisland sites, which have been supplied by The Dive Bunker. There is no need for guesswork: the sites are all there, waiting to be dived. Diving is an expensive business and this guide aims to ensure that you choose the right dive sites to maximise your enjoyment of the area. It also advises on conditions and warns you when certain sites should be avoided.

HOW TO GET THERE

Edinburgh is the nearest major city to the Firth of Forth and the dive sites around St Abbs and Eyemouth, so is the best place to aim for, offering all the sights and services that you would expect from Scotland's capital city. If, however you are purely interested in the sites around St Abbs and Eyemouth, Newcastle becomes a viable destination for travel by air or train.

By road from the south, travel north up the east coast on the A1, from which all the towns in this book are easy to find. Eyemouth, St. Abbs, Dunbar and North Berwick are all clearly signposted from the A1. For Fife and Burntisland, take the Edinburgh City by-pass and follow the signs for the Forth Bridge. As you cross the bridge, Deep Sea World is advertised at junction 1 of the M90, while for Burntisland, take junction 2 and head east, following the signs along the coast road for eight miles. From the west of Scotland, follow the M8 or appropriate route to Edinburgh and follow the signs to the Forth Road Bridge or City by-pass, picking up the A1 and continuing as above. From the north, pick up the M90 or appropriate road south to Edinburgh and continue as above.

Visitors by air can fly to Edinburgh, the most convenient option, or to Newcastle. Both airports offer hire car rentals.

Visitors by train can use any route to Edinburgh's Waverley station. Travelling from the south on the East Coast main line from England, trains stop at Berwick-upon-Tweed, Dunbar and occasionally at North Berwick, which is ideal if you have diving and accommodation booked there. North Berwick has a regular service to and from Edinburgh Waverley which takes around 30 minutes. Burntisland is also served by rail links from Edinburgh Waverley, with the bonus of taking you over the famous Forth Bridge.

If travelling by sea, Aberdeen, Rosyth, Newcastle upon Tyne and Hull are the nearest ferry ports to the area. Aberdeen and Hull are roughly four hours' drive from Edinburgh, while Rosyth is near Burntisland, just over the water in Fife. Newcastle is around two hours from Edinburgh.

WHERE TO STAY

Included in the dive centre information section of this book are dive charter operators in Eyemouth and St Abbs who offer accommodation as part of their dive package. While these are the facilities most commonly used by divers, as they are very conveniently located for the dive sites, all the areas mentioned in this book have a range of bed and breakfast accommodation and local guesthouses. And, if you wish to stay in a fancy hotel, Edinburgh has hundreds for you to choose from. Information on the type of accommodation you require can be obtained from the Scottish Tourist Board or at www.visitscotland.com

TIDES

There is, unfortunately, no easy fix for predicting slack water on the tides that rip through the Firth of Forth. The Inner Forth is strongly affected by the tidal flow of the River Forth. In the Outer Forth, where the estuary opens into the North Sea, the river's influence is minimal but sites closer to shore are affected by the drag caused by the shoreline. In short: if you are diving the sites in this book from your own boat, you will need to check an Admiralty chart to calculate slack water for the site that you wish to visit. I have included references to tidal information in those sites severely affected by the tide and where slack water is required to dive them safely or with any enjoyment.

There is, though, a very general rule of thumb which can be used to calculate roughly when slack water will occur. This has been supplied by Mark Blyth of The Dive Bunker for the Inner Forth and Jim and Iain Easingwood of Marine Quest for the Outer Forth.

In the Inner Forth, slack water on a spring tide will occur at high tide. Diving can be undertaken 30 minutes either side of high tide. On neap tides, the arrival of slack water is less precisely timed and can vary somewhat from the high tide time. High-tide slack is the preferred time to dive in the Inner Forth to ensure the best underwater visibility. This information relates to sites like the Blae Rock (dive site 6).

In the Outer Forth, slack water occurs around mid tide, i.e. three hours before and after high tide. This is in relation to wrecks such as *U-12* (dive site 94) situated well offshore. Further inshore, local conditions affect the time of slack water. Slack water for the *Glanmire* (dive site 61), for instance, is 2.5 hours after low water and three hours after high tide, whereas the *East Neuk* (dive site 97) experiences slack two hours after high and low tide.

As you can see, referring to the Admiralty chart is the only easy way of predicting slack water in the various sections of the Firth of Forth with any degree of accuracy.

I have not yet dived from the Forth Diving Services boat and can offer no comment on it. My experience of diving with all the other boats referred to in this book does, though, allow me to recommend their services, putting the diver on the chosen dive site when tidal influence is minimal.

DIVING QUALIFICATIONS EXPLAINED
REPRODUCED COURTESY OF THE BRITISH SUB AQUA CLUB

Aqualung Diving qualifications
(BSAC Branches may provide training for these qualifications to BSAC members only. BSAC Schools may award the BSAC Ocean Diver qualification ONLY to non-members, training for all other qualifications can be offered to BSAC members only).

OCEAN DIVER (known as CLUB Diver prior to September 2002) (Minimum age 12 years). A diver who is competent to dive with another Ocean Diver or Sports Diver, within restriction of conditions already encountered during training and can dive with a Dive Leader (or higher) to expand experience beyond conditions encountered during training. Ocean Divers will not have sufficient experience or knowledge to be partnered with trainee divers or take part in stage decompression stop dives. BSAC Ocean Divers are restricted to the maximum depth experienced during training (15 –20 m), which can be extended to a maximum of 20 m. Due to the limitations on their rescue skills, Ocean Divers can only conduct dives where other suitably-qualified divers who can act as surface support are present and the dive is properly marshalled to ensure that dives are conducted within BSAC Safe Diving Practice recommendations.

BSAC considers this qualification to be of a similar standard to CMAS One Star Diver.

SPORTS DIVER
A diver who is competent to dive with another Ocean Diver, within restriction of conditions already encountered during training and can dive with a Dive Leader (or higher) to expand experience beyond conditions encountered during training, under the supervision of a Dive Marshal. Sports Divers can dive with other Sports Divers within the restrictions of conditions already encountered during training or previous experience. Sports Divers are restricted to the maximum depth experienced during training (20 m) until qualified, but can subsequently extend this progressively under the supervision of an NQI to maximum depth of 35 m. Sports Divers will have sufficient experience or knowledge to conduct stage decompression stop dives and provide full rescue and CPR support and conduct dives within BSAC Safe Diving Practice recommendations.

BSAC considers this qualification to be of a similar standard to CMAS Two Star Diver.

DIVE LEADER
A diver who can plan and lead a range of dives and has the knowledge and skill to progressively extend both their own and others' experience. Dive Leaders are competent to marshal and supervise branch dives to locations well-known to the Branch or with experienced Charter Boat skippers and have the skills necessary to act as a Rescue manager. They can dive with any

grade of diver to expand their experience including trainee Ocean Divers, on dives supervised by a Dive Marshal.

ADVANCED DIVER

A diver who is comprehensively trained, experienced and responsible and can manage and supervise a wide range of adventurous and challenging diving. This will include organising expeditions to unknown locations and incorporating activities using developing technology. An Advanced Diver will take responsibility for ensuring that all dives are conducted within BSAC Safe Diving Practices. BSAC considers this qualification to be of a similar standard to CMAS Three Star Diver.

THE DIVER'S CODE OF CONDUCT
REPRODUCED COURTESY OF THE BRITISH SUB AQUA CLUB

More and more people are taking to the water; some for recreation; some to earn their living. This code is designed to ensure that divers do not come into conflict with other water users and sets out some guidelines which should be observed alongside the regulations relating to Marine Nature Reserves.

Before leaving home
Contact the nearest BSAC Branch or the dive operator local to the dive site for their advice. Seek advice from them about the local conditions and regulations. If appropriate, have the correct chart and tide tables for the area to be dived.

On the beach, river bank or lakeside
1.   Obtain permission before diving in a harbour or estuary or in private water. Thank those responsible before you leave. Pay harbour dues.
2.   Try to avoid overcrowding one site, consider other people on the beach.
3.   Park sensibly. Avoid obstructing narrow approach roads. Keep off verges. Pay parking fees and use proper car parks.
4.   Don't spread yourselves and your equipment since you may upset other people. Keep launching ramps and slipways clear.
5.   Please keep the peace. Don't operate a compressor within earshot of other people - or late at night.
6.   Pick up litter. Close gates. Be careful about fires. Avoid any damage to land or crops.
7.   Obey special instructions such as National Trust rules, local bye-laws and regulations about camping and caravanning.
8.   Remember divers in wet or drysuits are conspicuous and bad behaviour could ban us from beaches.

In and on the water
1.   Mark your dive boats so that your Club can be identified easily.

2. Ask the harbour-master or local officials where to launch your boat - and do as they say. Tell the Coastguard, or a responsible person, where you are going and tell them when you are back.
3. Stay away from buoys, pots, and pot markers. Ask local fishermen where not to dive. Avoid driving through rafts of seabirds or seal colonies etc.
4. Remember ships have not got brakes, so avoid diving in fairways or areas of heavy surface traffic and observe the 'International Regulations for the Prevention of Collisions at Sea'.
5. Always fly the diving flag when diving, but not when on the way to, or from, the dive site. Never leave a boat unattended.
6. Do not come in to bathing beaches under power. Use any special approach lanes. Do not disturb any seal or bird colonies with your boats. Watch your boat's wash in crowded anchorages.
7. Whenever possible, divers should use a surface marker buoy.

On conservation

1. Never use a speargun.
2. Shellfish, such as crabs and lobsters, take several years to grow to maturity; over-collecting in an area soon depletes stocks. Observe local Byelaws and restrictions on the collection of animal and plant specimens. However BSAC recommends that you do not collect shellfish, but if you must collect, only take mature fish or shellfish and then only what you need for yourself. Never take a berried female (a female with eggs), this is stock for future years. Never sell your catch or clean it in public or on the beach and do not display your trophies.
3. Ascertain and comply with seasonal access restrictions established to protect seabirds and seals from disturbance. During the seabird breeding season (1st March-1st August) reduce noise and speed near seabird breeding sites. Do not approach seal breeding or haul-out sites. Do not approach dolphins or porpoises in the water.
4. Be conservation conscious. Avoid damage to weeds and the sea bed. Do not bring up sea-fans, corals, starfish or sea urchins - in one moment you can destroy years of growth.
5. Take photographs and notes - not specimens.

On wrecks

1. Do not dive on a designated wreck site without a licence. Protected wrecks are indicated on Admiralty charts and marked by buoys, or warning notices on the shore nearby.
2. Military wrecks should not be disturbed or items removed from them. This includes the debris field. The debris field is the trail of wreckage that comes away from the main body of the wreck during the sinking process. This trail can consist of parts of the ship, the cargo and the personal possessions of the crew.
3. Do not lift anything that may be of archaeological importance.
4. If you do discover what might be an historic wreck do not talk about it, but contact the Receiver of Wreck (023 8032 9474), who will advise you about your next steps. If your find is important you may apply for it to be designated a protected wreck site. You can then build up a well-qualified team with the right qualifications to investigate your site with the assistance of a qualified archaeologist.

5. If you do lift any material from the sea-bed, it is a legal requirement to report it to the Receiver of Wreck as soon as reasonably possible; even if you own the wreck that the material has come from.

6. Avoid the temptation to take souvenirs. Go wreck diving to enjoy the scenery and life, or get involved in projects. If you must take something, try photographs or measurements, and records of marine life.

7. Know and understand wreck law. If you remove material from wreck, which you then sell for profit, you are diving for reward, which is outside the scope of sport diving and you must conduct your dives in strict accordance with HSE regulations. A sound knowledge of wreck law will prevent you breaking the law, perhaps even ending up with a criminal record where no crime was intended.

Members are reminded that in the light of this policy following any conviction of any BSAC member for an offence in relation to wreck the member will be liable to have his or her membership withdrawn for bringing BSAC into disrepute.

Don't let divers down - keep to the diver's code

The Divers Code of Conduct that is set out immediately above was developed by BSAC many years ago, and is still relevant to all divers today. However environmental issues are of greater concern to all water users today than ever before, particularly when this Code was developed, and so BSAC will be actively developing its environmental presence by the development of the following policies:-

To provide education in environmental awareness, understanding and enjoyment.

To promote Branch participation in environmental schemes and events.

Highlight current environmental issues, and work with other environmentalists in order to provide a united approach to deal with these issues.

To further develop and update the Divers Code of Conduct.

Policies of BSAC

Environmental

To make a sustained and positive impact to the freshwater and marine environment.

Respect our wrecks

Do not dive on a designated protected site, and do not lift anything that appears to be of historical interest.

Welfare of the vulnerable

Guidance to protect juvenile and vulnerable members of BSAC.

Copies of all of these policies are available from BSAC Headquarters.
For further details and information please contact
Diving Resources Department at BSAC Headquarters:
Tel: 44 (0) 151 350 6200   Fax: 44 (0) 151 350 6215
Website www.bsac.com   E-mail contacts: technical@bsac.com   membership@bsac.com

BURNTISLAND

Seven miles east of the Forth Bridge lies the small town of Burntisland. I remember as a boy being taken there on the train, to enjoy a day on the beach before moving on to the funfair in the park. This funfair still returns to the town every summer but I now visit purely for the diving. And while 'murky but magnificent' might sum up diving this far up the Firth of Forth, Burntisland does offer some thrilling dives. A wrecked aircraft carrier lies a mile offshore and an underwater pinnacle rises from 60 metres to just 12 metres below the surface. Visibility is not as good as it is further down the coast, but this more sheltered location provides diving in all but the worst of weather. Ten-metre visibility on the wrecks is a rarity here but is experienced by the lucky few.

The town of Burntisland itself is small but offers a few restaurants and bed-and-breakfasts. If you plan to dive and stay in this area, your first contact should be Mark Blyth of The Dive Bunker, who can advise you and help you plan your stay. The Dive Bunker conducts dives in their fast boats on all the local wrecks and reefs in this section.

Points of interest for families travelling in the area, besides the funfair in the summer months, are a leisure centre and swimming pool opposite the dive centre. Scotland's National Aquarium at Deep Sea World is eight miles away and the town of Dunfermline is just beyond. Here you will find the beautiful Pittencrieff Park and Dunfermline Palace and Abbey, the latter being the resting place of Robert the Bruce, King of Scots. The area also boasts quaint coastal villages along the Fife coast, with Edinburgh only 30 minutes away on the south side of the Firth of Forth.

Forth Bridge from North Queensferry

Deep Sea World sand tiger shark

Dive no. 1

Name
Deep Sea World

Location
North Queensferry, Fife

Depth
0–6 metres

Conditions
Dark, clear, calm water

Access
Easy

Diver experience
Ocean diver (no diving experience required)

Dive site

Deep Sea World, or Scotland's National Aquarium, is a little bit different from the dives which follow in this book. This large complex is just east of the Forth Bridge and is well signposted and easy to find. The site covers two levels, and offers the visitor the chance to see tropical coral reefs and displays from the Amazon as well as touch pools on the upper level. Of more interest to divers, though, is the million-litre aquarium on the lower floor, filled with fish found around the UK and sand tiger sharks that thrive quite happily in the water fed from the Firth of Forth.

For me, diving withdrawal symptoms start to bite in February and March, when the weather is at its worst in the Firth of Forth, and I have recently found myself making a pilgrimage to Deep Sea World for a shark dive. It's great to start the year underwater surrounded by hundreds of fish in this sheltered environment. Visibility is around 20 metres, as the water is constantly filtered, and for the sake of the sand tiger sharks, the temperature is never allowed to drop below 10 degrees Celsius. It really is exciting to get into the water with them, and they seem a lot larger through the glass of the mask than through the curved perspex lens of the aquarium's underwater walkway, from where non-diving visitors view the exhibit. There are tope and angel sharks to be seen too, with a variety of rays, mackerel, bass and bream buzzing past. I remember a large female conger eel doing laps of the aquarium, her biological clock telling her that she should be spawning in the Sargasso Sea. (The aquarium no longer houses conger eels as, once this behaviour has been displayed, the eel will die even if released immediately back into the wild.) The main tank does now contain fewer exhibits than in previous years and sadly there are no longer any wreckfish, sturgeon, sea trout or skate, although I hope they'll be restocked one day, as they make a really interesting sight. There is still plenty to see, however, once you get used to bouncing along the floor, picking a patch of sand not occupied by a big turbot or ray to progress around the tank, as fins are not worn in the aquarium. It is fairly easy, apart from when you have to jump over the large perspex viewing tunnel, and very exciting. I have dived in the aquarium on a number of occasions, the sharks sometimes keeping their distance and at other times coming quite close, which of course makes for much better photographs. There is very little available light in the aquarium so photography can be challenging, but the fish do come close, so a flash will get some amazing results.

It's a great place to dive and I thoroughly recommend it. To be so close to big sharks is a thrilling and unforgettable experience.

Dive nights are priced at £65 per person or you can make extra savings by booking as a group. You can find further information about dive nights at www.sharkdives. deepseaworld.com. This is also a site that you could turn to if you arrive for a dive trip to find conditions impossible in the Firth of Forth.

Dive no. 2

Name
Grumman Avenger

Location
Burntisland
No GPS coordinates available

Contact
The Dive Bunker to arrange a dive

Depth
12–14 metres

Conditions
Very tidal, slack water required. Visibility generally 3–5 metres

Access
Boat only

Diver experience
Sports diver

The Dive Bunker's new RIB

Dive site
This aircraft is far too modern to have run down the flight deck of HMS *Campania* (dive site 4). It was land-based and operated out of Crail airfield. While on a training flight on 17 December 1945, just after the end of hostilities, the big Wright r-2600

14-cylinder, double-row cyclone engine started to give the pilot cause for concern. Ditching the aircraft in the Firth of Forth in December must have been a very unwelcome prospect, but in all my research, I have found no mention of the crew and it does appear that they all survived. The wreck is certainly not classed as a war grave.

Today the wreck lies in 12–14 metres of water. Out of the gloom, the forward part of the aircraft materialises and the two large propeller blades that rise up from the seafloor appear to make an anemone-encrusted 'V for Victory'. I was surprised by the size of the prop, which was much larger than I had expected. The cylinders in the radial engine are all there to be seen and, further back, the fuselage is mainly intact and excellently preserved. Further aft, the cockpit canopy is missing, perhaps lost in the crew's rush to get out of the aircraft. The wings spread out over the mud and a good amount of marine life thrives on the wreck. The machine gun blister lies off the wreck in the sand but otherwise everything is intact. A diver reportedly raised the machine gun in an attempt to identify the aircraft, yet it was not this piece of salvage, but records of ditched aircraft that identified it as a Grumman-built TBF-1B Avenger torpedo bomber, also known as the Tarpon when delivered to the Fleet Air Arm. The Fleet Air Arm during the war received almost a thousand of these aircraft as part of the Lend-Lease agreement and the Grumman Avenger was to become the chief carrier-based torpedo bomber of the Royal Navy. It outperformed the previous carrier aircraft, the Barracuda and Fairey Swordfish, which then became obsolete.

This aircraft was found while HMS *Roebuck* was surveying the Firth of Forth with a ground-penetrating radar, carrying out an exercise to search for the remains of King Charles I's treasure ship. Anomalies needed to be clarified, and the Avenger and a Hurricane were two of the aircraft wrecks that were found and dived.

A compass was also raised from the wreck and is now on display at the Burntisland Museum, while the machine gun was sent to the National Museum of Flight just east of Edinburgh. Both artefacts were declared to the Receiver of Wreck. Today, though, there is a strict 'no touch' policy on this fragile but historically important site.

Herring drifter

Dive no. 3

Name
Unknown 'Woodbine' steam herring drifter

Location
Out from Burntisland
GPS coordinates N56028.90
W03002.49

Depth
20 metres

Conditions
Dark water. Expect visibility of around 3 metres

Access
Boat only

Diver experience
Sports Diver/Dive Leader

Dive site
This is a fantastic wee wreck of a type of vessel that used to ply the Firth of Forth in their hundreds, if not thousands. I was dropped onto this newly-found wreck, which sits bolt upright in 20 metres of water, by Mark Blyth, owner of The Dive Bunker at Burntisland. The visibility at this site is likely to be poor: I experienced 3 metres visibility and I would expect this to be the average. The wreck is by no means dull, however, with extremely large plumose anemones in their usual orange-and-white coloration brightening up the rusty steel. Descending onto the bow, large capstans are visible, while further aft are the remains of a small wheelhouse and some superstructure. Then comes one of the vessels most distinctive features, the large, rounded, sloping stern which, to the diver underneath it, seems to go on forever until eventually the propeller comes into view. My brief investigation led me to conclude that this was a steam drifter most likely to have been used to fish for herring. This type of vessel filled the ports of the Firth of Forth at the turn of the 20th century. These vessels were nicknamed 'Woodbine', in reference to their long, thin funnel designed to keep the harmful engine smoke away from the men tending their nets at the stern and looking very much like a smoking cigarette. In an era when sail was giving way to new steam-powered vessels, the funnel was probably the most interesting feature to any inquisitive passers-by, strolling along the quayside. It makes me smile to think about the fishermen, there on the stern, working the nets and no doubt puffing on

Woodbines, yet protected from the engine smoke of this new type of vessel by its long thin funnel.

This once most common of ships is now lost to history, with only a very few examples remaining afloat. I did not see the remains of the funnel on my brief visit to this most interesting wreck and would like to return to the site to see what survives of it.

Diver explores wreck

Dive no. 4

Name
HMS *Campania*

Location
Inner Firth of Forth, one mile off Burntisland
GPS coordinates N56024.27 W03134.25

Depth
14–30 metres

Conditions
Visibility variable but usually poor at 2–6 metres

Access
Boat only. Contact The Dive Bunker

Diver experience
Sports diver

Dive site

HMS *Campania* started life as RMS *Campania*, a new luxury liner for the Cunard Line. At 12,884 tonnes she was the first of the luxury liners as we think of them today. Her impressive speed meant that she was converted into an aircraft carrier and was written into the history books as the first carrier to launch a plane from the flight deck whilst underway. These facts, though, are only a very small part of this magnificent ship's history. This vessel, designated as a special site of interest, is one of the most famous shipwrecks that you will ever dive.

A wreck of this size in a shipping channel as busy as the Firth of Forth obviously didn't last long. Images taken immediately after the sinking show the *Campania* resting on a relatively even keel, with funnels and mast protruding from the surface. It would have made a magnificent dive, but this massive wreck was a serious hazard to navigation and charges were set along her famous flight deck.

What remains today, though, is still extremely impressive. Side-scan sonar images show the remains generally lying on the starboard side, the bow clearly defined and structures, such as the funnels and cranes, identifiable. Divers will note that the water is green and relatively clear until 14 metres, at which point it turns black. The wreck lies on a muddy seafloor at a maximum depth of 30 metres and rises up to a height of 14 metres, it is still a serious dive. Landing on the seafloor at around 24 metres in two-metre visibility, the diver finds a wall of steel rising up at an angle above them in a relatively intact section of the wreck, which must be near the bow. Portholes rising up this wall of steel and mud make posh pads for lobsters to lie up in. A sparse covering of dead man's fingers, sea urchins and brittle stars cover the hull here, but this changes as the diver rises to deck level, where railings and everything else is covered in a dense carpet of plumose anemones. The total colonisation of the wreck by marine life means that even studying models of HMS *Campania* to try to identify your position won't help much. I could not tell masts from guns when I dived this wreck, as the structures were so big and the visibility on the day was so low. I know the guns are there, as she sank in a fighting state, but I was unable to make any kind of definite identification. I could, however, identify smaller items such as bollards, portholes and sections of anchor chain. Finning along, monster lion's mane jellyfish make a nuisance of themselves in the summer months, so do watch out for them, as the swarms of these big stingers get quite dense. Dropping down the practically vertical deck, back onto the seafloor at around 24 metres, I looked back and saw the big structures back-lit by surface light, valiantly filtering down through the murk. Exploring the deck in this area, a large structure can be seen, perhaps one of the cranes used for lifting the aircraft, while further aft, one of the *Campania*'s distinctive funnels is on display. Rising back up the deck, the diver soon finds railings adorned by orange-and-white plumose anemones and drifting lion's mane jellyfish. This point, nearing the end of the dive, is a good opportunity to send up a delayed surface marker buoy (DSMB) and start the ascent back into the light.

This is a monster wreck at just under 200 metres long and a number of dives to see it in sections could help give the bigger picture. I was lucky enough to get back onto this wreck when the visibility was 6 metres, and, with luck, 10 metres is possible.

Knowing a little of *Campania*'s history will help put this impressive wreck into context for the diver. In 1892, RMS *Campania* became the first steamship of the Cunard Fleet to be fitted with twin propellers. Although this was a first for Cunard, their rivals, Inman & International Line, had introduced twin screws on their North Atlantic-run steamships, *City of New York* and *City of Paris*. It would be these ships' only victory over *Campania* as they were outclassed in every other department.

On 22 April 1893, RMS *Campania* made her maiden voyage from Liverpool to New York and all went well. On the return leg, *Campania* set a record for the fastest crossing of the Atlantic and gained the Blue Riband for the first time. *Campania* and her sister, *Lucania*, dominated the field until the German liner, Norddeutscher Lloyd's *Kaiser*

Wilhelm der Grosse, took the record in 1897. The Blue Riband was associated with the strength of a nation and this ship heralded Germany's intent: she was strengthening her fleet. That year, the *Campania* represented Cunard at Queen Victoria's Diamond Jubilee review at Spithead, sailing between massed lines of battleships, reflecting the shape of things to come.

For the next three years, *Campania* continued her fast, reliable crossings of the Atlantic until a serious accident in July 1900. *Campania* collided with the barque *Embelton*, slicing the smaller ship in two. Eleven lives were lost when the bow section sank immediately.

The next year, the advent of wireless communication brought with it another first for *Campania* and *Lucania*, the first vessels to be fitted with and to use a Marconi wireless telegraph. However, in October 1905, disaster struck: a huge wave hit *Campania*, sweeping five steerage passengers overboard to their deaths and injuring 29 others when it burst through the steerage compartment doors.

By 1907, Germany had dominated the high seas for a decade. The next generation of Cunards were launched, in the form of the *Lusitania* and *Mauretania*. They made an immediate impact and would go on to become famous in their own right.

It was World War One that saved the ageing *Campania* from the scrapyard. She was on her way there when the Admiralty stepped in with visionary plans for the old speed queen. She was to be transformed from a beautiful liner into the world's first aircraft carrier, and went on to make history by launching the first aircraft from her flight deck whilst underway. *Campania* missed the Battle of Jutland in 1918, although she was anchored in Scapa Flow, as she was too slow to catch up with the rest of the fleet, a cruel twist of fate for this once most speedy of ships. She headed south to Burntisland in the Firth of Forth. Here, on 5 November 1918, in a terrible storm, *Campania* dragged her anchor and ran across the bows of a battleship. The identity of the battleship is unclear but three names keep coming up: *Royal Oak, Revenge* and *Glorious*.

The *Campania* was fatally holed and started to settle by the stern, her blue-and-white dazzle paint slowly slipping below the surface. She had missed surviving the war by four days and suffered an inglorious end for such a magnificent ship.

HMS Saucy *diver and bow gun*

Dive no. 5

Name
HMS *Saucy*

Location
Mid-forth, 2 km west of
Inchkeith Island
GPS coordinates N56021.98
W03108.15

Depth
17–24 metres

Conditions
Moderate visibility, slack water
dive only

Access
Boat launch from Burntisland, Newhaven or Granton

Diver experience
Sports diver

Dive site
Search and Rescue tugs such as HMS *Saucy* played an important role in World War
Two, recovering sailors from sunken vessels and pilots from downed aircraft. These tugs
were crewed by merchant seamen and fishermen rather than by Royal Navy personnel.
On 3 September 1940, HMS *Saucy* had just completed a mission when she struck a
mine 2.5 kilometres west of Inchkeith Island. The stern section was blown completely
off the ship and she sank very quickly. Twenty six men lost their lives (many of whom
were from Brixham in Devon), just five survived. In Leith's Seafield cemetery are the
beautifully-tended graves of the eight victims whose bodies were recovered.

HMS *Saucy* has a sad history, like any ship lost in an act of violence. Today, though,
she lies as a beautiful wreck and, I think, a fitting resting place for the missing sailors.
Needless to say, this site is a war grave and should be treated with the utmost respect.

This little tug makes a fantastic dive. The forward section of the wreck is completely
intact, anchors hanging in their hawse pipes adorned by plumose anemones. These fight
a raging battle with colonies of small dahlia anemones which have their home on the
flukes of the anchor. I noted that one of these anemones was devouring the claw of a
velvet-backed swimming crab. Dropping down to the seafloor at around 23 metres,
the bow of the *Saucy* is raised well off the seabed, where a large scour has been created,
allowing an intrepid diver to pass under the bow if they wish to do so. On the muddy
seafloor at the base of the bow, the diver can marvel at the straight line of the bow
rising up over 4 metres to the prow. It's adorned all the way in that never-ending carpet

of plumose anemones. Rising back up to deck level, a huge winch comes into view. Anchor chains run out to the hawse pipes and mooring bollards can also be made out. Further back there is a large spray guard and the barrel of the deck gun emerges from the gloom. Here rages another battle, this time between a colony of white plumose anemones inhabiting the breech end of the gun and an orange clump that inhabits the business end of the barrel. There is a distinct border of rusty steel between the two warring factions. The muzzle of the gun is angled up slightly, pointing to the surface. This will be many a diver's favourite part of the wreck and in good visibility it makes a stunning sight. Visibility will be in the range of 0–10 metres with an average of around 5 metres, which is fairly good considering that this wreck lies in the inner Firth of Forth. Just aft of the breech of the gun, a small rectangular hole, like a letterbox, can be seen in the deck: this is where the spent shell cases were placed. Finning further back, the bridge rises up from deck level. The whole structure of the wreck is carpeted in plumose anemones. I don't think I have ever been on wrecks that have such dense coverings of soft corals as do these wrecks in the Firth of Forth. It certainly makes for a colourful sight when backed by the green water. Even in poorer conditions, light still penetrates the murky water down to the deck at 17 metres. Finning further aft behind the bridge, HMS *Saucy* starts to lose her shape a little, thanks to the magnetic mine that sent her to the bottom. There are still many recognisable features, such as crates of ammunition for the deck gun, silted-up stairways leading to the innards of this war grave and, beneath a light coating of silt, two brass skylights gleam in the diver's torch beam. The remains of masts and ventilation shafts are still visible and one of *Saucy*'s funnels can clearly be seen, lying across the wooden deck in a remarkable state of preservation. The hull finally does break just forward of the stern and there is a pile of debris inhabited by massive lobsters and edible crabs. Here there are openings and doorways that allow the diver to glimpse inside the hull and to view what must have been the ship's engine room. The stern section now lies around 100 metres from the main wreck, proof of the massive damage caused to the ship and of the speed with which she sank after the explosion. This section of the wreck has only recently been located as it was originally thought that the whole stern section had been destroyed in the explosion.

This is an extremely colourful and scenic wreck completely encrusted with soft corals. Lion's mane jellyfish are also extremely common in early summer. With a background of green water, it makes a beautiful sight. Lying in a tidal part of the estuary, slack water is the preferred time to dive this wreck, as the tide runs across the deck and can be strong enough to wash a diver off. Neap tides are also desirable as the muddy seafloor is affected by tidal movement and the smallest tides generally provide the best visibility.

There is a very informative website dedicated to the men from Brixham and elsewhere who lost their lives on HMS *Saucy*. This little armed tug certainly has an interesting history and a simple internet search under 'Brixham Memorials' will provide a great deal more information about her and her crew.

Blae Rock diver with common jellyfish

Dive no. 6

Name
Blae Rock

Location
One mile out of Burntisland
GPS coordinates N56030.08
W03114.06

Depth
12–60 metres

Conditions
Extreme diving conditions,
downcurrents. Best dived at
slack water on neap tide

Tidal information
Slack water window will occur
between one hour before high
water at Leith to 45 minutes
after high water (on neap tides).
On spring tides, slack water will
occur around high tide. Very
short window avoid ebb tide.

Access
Boat only

Diver experience
Sports diver/dive leader

Dive site
This dive should get your pulses
racing. A massive pinnacle of
rock, the size of a football field, rises straight up from more than 60 metres to 12 metres from the surface. It's a massive obstruction to the flow of the tide in the Firth of
Forth. The big tankers that ply the Forth give the Blae Rock a wide berth as the tide
does strange things here, so it is a slack water dive. The Blae makes a fantastic dive, some
say the best scenic dive on the southeast coast of Scotland. I would say it's certainly the
most exciting scenic dive on this coast, and even if it's not my personal favourite, it's
certainly in my top ten. After all, only the Bass Rock has a big wall to challenge this
site. The tide is critical to complete this dive safely and neap tides are best. They will
allow novice divers to enjoy the colonies of brittle stars, schools of pollack and dinner-

plate sized dahlia anemones of every colour that grace the top of the pinnacle without fear of being washed off the top or, worse, sucked over the cliff face. Neap tides will also enable more experienced divers to reach the site's very impressive cliffs. To find the cliffs, head west down gullies where, at a depth of 20–26 metres, the big cliff drops away vertically to more than 60 metres. In good visibility this is a stunning sight and going over the edge really is adrenaline-pumping stuff. Hexagonal basalt columns plummet down into the depths and large cracks run up the walls providing a home for lobsters, Yarrel's blennies, conger eels, and I have even seen a wolffish here. The walls are covered in dead man's fingers and large colonies of plumose anemones which thrive in the tidal water. I noted pairs of golden eyes belonging to large prawns, hiding among the anemones and reflecting back my torchlight.

Levelling off at just over 30 metres is a good depth to enjoy the wall, as finning south at this depth takes you under ledge after ledge of impressive overhangs. Visibility at this site is a mercurial business. The site is in the estuary and the smaller tides do provide the best visibility which can be good even in the early season. This far up the Forth you are sheltered from the big gales that often make the east coast of Scotland undiveable. I have experienced visibility of around 5 metres and would expect this to be the average, although I have dived the site in bright water with awesome 10-metre visibility. That said, I've also been sucked over the top of the cliff in 1 metre visibility. It's definitely exciting diving.

Dive no. 7

Vows Reef pink shrimp

Name
Vows Reef

Location
Between Kinghorn and
Kirkcaldy, directly offshore from Seafield Tower, and the furthest rock offshore

Depth
13 metres maximum

Conditions
Easy. Little tide, average
visibility 5 metres

Access
Boat only

Diver experience
Ocean diver

Dive site
It's very likely that you will never have heard of this little site, unless, that is, you have been a dive student of The Dive Bunker, as this is their training site. The small group of rocks that form the Vows are home to grey seals, and I counted seven of them having a good look at us as the boat pulled up to the site. The seals, being inquisitive creatures, will often join divers for a play underwater as well.

The boat is always anchored inshore of the islands as this is the most sheltered point of entry for new divers. It's a fin of around 50 metres over to the rocks. The seafloor is sand with seams of coal pebbles floating on top, proof of the rich coalfields that run out from the Fife coast under the Firth of Forth. It's likely that the miners' tunnels dug to extract the coal run right out to sea under the dive site too. On the inside of the reef the depth is 6 metres. As you near the rocks, patches of kelp will become apparent and the wall will appear as a barrier in front of you. To experience the best dive, you'll need to cross over to the offshore side of the reef. Do this by looking for a small amphitheatre in which you will find a small gully, allowing you to fin through the rock and emerge on the outer reef. The depth here quickly drops away to 12 metres. At the base of the wall is a patch of sand, and a reef of around 1 metre in height then rises out of the seafloor. The rock is heavily fissured, with horizontal crevices running along the reef which runs for over 600 metres in a northerly direction. It is packed full of marine life, laid out like products in a supermarket, just waiting for you to come and inspect them. Crustaceans are the most notable residents, northern prawns pack the shelves, along with lobsters. Large edible crabs are found here too but they prefer the sand at the base of the reef or the layer of seaweed on top of the rocks. I once found a monster specimen here and managed to rattle off a few shots while the crab just sat there for the camera. Velvet-backed swimming crabs are also prevalent here but they are much more flighty and will not keep still unless they feel secure in one of the recesses in the reef. It's not just shellfish though: look closely and you will find gobies and flatfish in the pebbles at the base of the reef. Pipefish are also a common sight here and dahlia anemones brighten up the scene with their vibrant colours. The depth stays constant once you reach the outer reef with a max of around 13 metres. It's nice to fin along for an hour, taking in all the natural sights. At the northern end of the reef is a man-made point of interest in the form of a shipwreck. This was the *Adam Smith* and its remains lie off the offshore side of the rocks, 400 metres north of the Vows. The remains include anchors and a large winch as well as lots of steel plating and anchor chain that lie at the base of the rock, while the ship's boiler and propeller lie just offshore on the sandy seafloor.

The Vows is a pretty little dive which macro-photographers will enjoy. This certainly is not a boring little training site, but rather a great scenic site in its own right. The scenery is unlike anything I had dived before.

Dive no. 8

Divers explore wreck of unknown trawler

Name
Unknown trawler

Location
Out of Burntisland

GPS unavailable. See the dive bunker to arrange dive

Depth
27 metres

Conditions
Muddy sea floor, average visibility 3 metres

Access
Boat only

Diver experience
Sports diver

Dive site
This wooden wreck is, as usual, completely covered in soft corals but there were large surfaces of metal which I found hard to explain. A large propeller was visible at the stern and a large green box, similar to an ammunition box, was reported to be lying off the bow, so the wreck became more and more intriguing. However, a second dive in slightly better conditions, with 3-metre visibility, confirmed that this was most likely a wooden fishing trawler lying hull-up and partially buried in the sea floor. The

metal is thought to be water or fuel tanks and the interesting green box at the bow turned out to be nothing more than part of the wooden hull which had broken off, the remaining green paint from the hull making it look more interesting than it really was. The propeller certainly looks large for the amount of hull that remains exposed, so this wreck does remain a complete mystery and I have no clue as to its identity. One thing I do know, though: it's certainly not King Charles I's treasure ship, which remains elusive.

There are better sites to visit in this area and, with a depth of 27 metres, I would suggest that this site will only interest divers wanting to chalk up a new wreck, or somebody wanting to identify the vessel.

Sylvestria *wreckage*

Dive no. 9

Name
Salvestria

Location
3 miles north of Inchkeith Island
GPS coordinates N5604.06 W0304.85

Depth
23–27 metres

Conditions
Flattened wreck

Access
Boat only

Diver experience
Sports Diver

Dive site
The *Salvestria* is one of those wrecks that make you wish they had sunk a little deeper, or out of the main shipping channel. She was a massive 12,000-gross ton vessel, over 150 metres long, and would have made a superb dive had she still been intact. Purchased in 1929 by Christian

Salvesen, she was converted into a whale processing vessel, similar in design, if older, to the Japanese Nisshin Maru which attracts protest nowadays from anti-whaling groups. During World War Two, the *Salvestria* operated as a tanker, carrying fuel oil rather than whale oil, and it was while carrying out this duty with a full cargo of fuel oil that she struck a mine, just north of Inchkeith Island. Ten men lost their lives in the massive explosion. The *Salvestria* quickly slipped beneath the waves, polluting the Firth of Forth with her cargo of oil. She sat almost totally intact underwater until she was heavily salvaged and then completely dispersed with depth charges. What remains on the seafloor is a completely flattened wreck. The steel plates that formed her hull have been twisted into unrecognisable shapes. It's not a pretty sight, especially in the murky brown water found in the upper Firth of Forth near Inchkeith Island. This is where the estuary narrows and visibility deteriorates to around 3 metres. The only highlight of my dive was a porthole, trapped where it lay, but more recent artefacts are often found here: the anchors of small vessels, entangled in the wreckage and lost as the boats fished over the site. There is also deposits of fishing tackle. Perhaps the *Salvestria* is better left for anglers as her remains make for a bland dive. Dive her if she is a new wreck for you and you'd like her name in your logbook, but not even the possibility of finding a porthole intact would lure me back for a second visit. There are far better wrecks to be explored in the Firth of Forth.

Royal Archer *divers with ship's bell*

Dive no. 10

Name
Royal Archer

Location
Southeast of Kirkcaldy
Gps coordinates N56064.49
W03001.09

Depth
31 metres

Conditions
Large shipwreck

Access
Boat only

Diver experience
Dive leader

Dive site
The *Royal Archer* was in sight of

the port of Leith on what turned out to be her final voyage in 1940 and she almost made it safely to dock, but instead became a casualty of war. She did make it slightly further up the Firth of Forth that did her sister ship, the *Royal Fusilier* (dive entry 20), which sank east of the Bass Rock after being bombed by German aircraft. The *Royal Archer* fell victim to a mine deployed by the German submarine *U-21*. Lying in depths of 27–31 metres, depending on the tide, the remains of the *Royal Archer* are generally flattened. The stern is now the most intact area of the wreck, standing almost 4 metres proud of the seafloor and with recognisable features. Anemone-encrusted railings still surround the stern and a fire hose reel and mooring bollards decorate the decking of this small, intact section of the wreck. The propeller and rudder are either hidden from view in the mud or may perhaps have been salvaged. This wreck can be a pretty dive as the rusty steel, particularly around the stern, is covered in orange-and-white dead man's fingers. Plumose anemones are present, reflecting the more tidal location of the wreck. Visibility is also superior here compared with the wrecks further up the Firth of Forth, with the average visibility being around 8 metres. Schools of bib are found here, as well as the more common pollack, while massive lobsters can be seen amongst the broken wreckage and beneath the stern. The midships area is broken and the engine and boilers appear to have been salvaged, or possibly flattened and obscured by the piles of wreckage that once was this smart steamship. Interesting items of her cargo are still to be seen, though, notably the chassis and axles of trucks, still fitted with wheels and tyres. It's also good to know that there are still a lot of non-ferrous items to be seen on this wreck: some of the large brass portholes are partially trapped under the wreckage and I have seen a brass fuel cap of some sort on the deck. Most recently though, even though this wreck has been heavily dived, the bell was raised by Emma Smith and the owner of The Dive Bunker, Mark Blyth. Mark frequently puts his customers on this impressive wreck, placing the shotline in the same position, so hundreds of divers have finned over the bell, unaware of its presence. It was found by a stroke of good luck. Part of it was sticking out of the seabed and was spotted by Emma as soon as she reached the seafloor, while Mark secured the shotline to the wreck. After a considerable amount of digging to free the bell, which weighs around 20 kg, Mark managed to rope it off and bring it safely to the surface. Having seen the raised bell myself, it's obvious which section of it has been protected and preserved by being buried. This is an interesting wreck with good amounts of marine life, and is certainly a good site for those divers wishing to build up to 30-metre diving.

NORTH BERWICK

No matter where you are in the Firth of Forth, the volcanic pyramid of Berwick Law can be seen. Its summit is just under 200 metres in height and is crowned with the jawbones of a whale. It is the largest of the many volcanic outcrops in the area and it makes a dominating landmark. Further to the east is the massive volcanic plug known as the Bass Rock. This island and three others like it form a straight line which points directly to the famous Castle Hill in Edinburgh, 20 miles away, which is the western-most volcanic plug of the chain.

From a diving point of view, the four islands in this chain are of great interest. These are, from east to west, the Bass Rock, Craigleith, Lamb and Fidra. They provide some of the most exciting and scenic dives to be found in southeast Scotland. All have an individual character and divers of all levels will find something to suit them.

To reach these islands, North Berwick is the best place to start. A wide slipway used by the RNLI station is available, leading onto a firm sandy beach where boats can be launched. Please note, however, that parking is difficult here, as it also is around the harbour. Divers have in the past been asked to move their cars even if using a hard boat from the harbour and that's not much fun if you use a twin set. If you have a trolley, do use it. There is a parking area at the harbour, on the site of the former open-air pool, but this appears to be used for yachts, and it would be good to see better facilities for divers using this harbour.

Parking aside, North Berwick is a delightful seaside town, very popular with visi-tors form Edinburgh at the weekends. It's a pleasant place to spend a day and it has fantastic sandy beaches. The Scottish SeaBird Centre is an interesting attraction and the town also boasts a nice park. Some very impressive castles are found very close to North Berwick and if you are at all interested in history, you should make a point of visiting Tantallon Castle to the east and Dirleton Castle to the west. Berwick Law makes an interesting climb for the fit, but not after diving. Slightly further west, at Aberlady Bay, taking a walk at low tide can reveal two midget submarines (see dive site 11).

There are a small number of bed-and-breakfasts, caravan parks, pubs and restaurants available in North Berwick. Edinburgh is 20 miles to the west.

North Berwick with Craigleith Island

Dive no. 11

XT-craft

Name
XT-craft (midget submarines)

Location
Aberlady bay

Depth
0 metres

Conditions
Superb wrecks

Access
Low tide access via aberlady nature reserve. Car park after double s bend after passing through Aberlady on the road to Gullane

Diver experience
No diving experience required

Dive site
Should you ever find that your planned dive is cancelled by adverse weather condition, this site is fantastic and offers two very special wrecks as an alternative. The XT-craft found here are the training versions of the X-craft midget submarine, used to attack the German battleship *Tirpitz* in a Norwegian fjord in 1942.

This is a dry dive and requires a walk of 1.5 miles to the submarines. Low tide is essential to enjoy the site for as long as possible. There are two XT-craft at the site, used as gunnery practice targets and moored 100 metres either side of a very large concrete block. You'll find the site by looking out for the block, which is much more visible from a distance than are the subs themselves. The more southerly submarine is in a better state of preservation.

These training versions of the X-craft differed in a number of ways from the operational models. the main difference being the wet/dry airlock compartment, used by the boat's diver to exit the sub while the vessel was underwater. On the training variants, only a standard escape hatch was fitted.

On the way out, stop in the nature reserve car park to take a look at the memorial to the Scots' historical fiction author Nigel Tranter. One day, Nigel was out in the bay hoping to shoot a goose, using one of the subs as a hide. When the tide turned and the sea surged in, Nigel found that he was trapped in the sub and needed to use the barrels of his shotgun to lever the hatch open and escape. He died in 2000 and this clearly seemed the most fitting place in which to set his memorial.

Leaving the car park, cross the bridge over the Peffer Burn and follow the path, passing a pond which is always worth a look, full of spawning frogs in April and May. Further on is a sewage treatment plan, identified by hundreds of crows flying around it. Near here the path splits, so take the footpath to the left towards the sand. This path is well signposted: just follow it straight out and over a dune. In the distance stands Cockenzie power station and lining up its two chimneys will lead you directly to the subs. You should by now be able to see the large concrete block that tethered them. Good walking boots or wellies will be enough to deal with the pools which you may have to splash through, but it is mainly firm sand. The first sub will be found after 300 metres. The changing sands here always reveal buried items. When I last visited the wrecks I came across the remains of a wartime jeep buried in the sand and there are also the hulks of a few large wooden trawlers at the low water mark. To return to the car park, just retrace your route. This is a great site in beautiful surroundings and allows you, if bad weather strikes, still to sign off two new wrecks without even getting wet.

Diver explores wreck of **Chester II**

Dive no. 12

Name
Chester II

Location
West of North Berwick
GPS coordinates N5604.26
W0252.31

Depth
28 metres maximum

Conditions
Silty wreck. Expect visibility of around 4 metres

Access
Boat only

Diver experience
Experienced sports diver

Dive site

The *Chester II* lies completely upright on a silty seafloor. This wreck certainly suffers if a full boatload of divers is dropped onto it, as the visibility soon deteriorates, but if you have the chance to dive it, don't let this fact put you off. The *Chester II* is a good wreck. While you should never rush to ready your dive gear, I would nonetheless recommend that you start preparing your gear five minutes earlier than usual. If you are completely ready to go when the shotline goes onto the wreck, the effort will be worth it, ensuring that you experience the best conditions.

The wreck is festooned with large orange-and-white plumose anemones and is in an intact state. Dropping down onto the stern of the wreck, good buoyancy control will minimise the silt storm on landing. The start of the dive is a good time to drop over the side to have a look at the rudder and prop shaft, although the propeller has been removed from the wreck. There are large sections of rope here so do take care. Rising back up to deck level, the diver will enjoy the marine life which encrusts everything. Mooring bollards are visible as are two arch-like structures behind the wheelhouse, perhaps some form of trawl gear. The wheelhouse itself is intact and small entrances lead into the dark interior. Moving forward past the wheelhouse, the small silt-filled holds can be seen. A gun mount remains on the deck, forward of the holds although, sadly, the gun has been lifted off the wreck. Further forward, just aft of the bows, a large winch can be seen. The wreck is small and shallow and enables divers to meander back to the shotline taking in the sights, possibly finning around the other side of the wheelhouse. This wreck may be a bit dark and silty but the masses of colourful anemones and the wreck's intact state make the *Chester II* a wonderful dive.

Rolfsborg *diver exploring wreck*

Dive no. 13

Name
Rolfsborg

Location
3.5 miles southwest of Elie, Fife
GPS coordinates N5608.27
W0252.06

Depth
Seabed 50 metres. Wreck rises
to above 40 metres

Conditions
Fantastic intact wreck. Visibility
variable, 2–8 metres

Access
Boat only

Diver experience
Advanced diver/technical diver

Dive site
The *Rolfsborg* is a magnificent wreck and completely under-dived. She rises up from a seafloor of 50 metres and rises up above 40 metres. The wreck is in a wonderful state of preservation and is quite intact. She sank on colliding with the steamship *Empire Swordsman* in 1945, just after the end of the war. I have read a few reports which incorrectly state that the wreck is lying on its port side and mentioning a large brass eagle decorating her stern. When I dived this wreck I obviously wanted to see the eagle. I descended, hit the deck, turned right and arrived not at the stern, but at the bow, so can guarantee that the *Rolfsborg* is lying on her starboard side. As for the brass eagle, I have yet to see it, but it may well be there. Two of my three dives on this wreck had to be aborted. The first was diving from a trawler out from Fife and the dive turned out to be on the seabed near the *Rolfsborg*. The second attempt was a fantastic dive, while on the third my main light failed. A back-up torch and my camera lights were not enough for more than a short dive on the route I knew around the bow. I will have to return to this wreck for a bit of underwater bird-watching.

A dive on the *Rolfsborg* is an interesting experience. When you arrive at the now near-vertical deck, keep the deck on your left shoulder to reach the bow. Poor visibility at the site is one of the main reasons this wreck is under-dived, and visibility in the region of 5 metres is considered to be good. The wreck has been completely colonised by orange plumose anemones, and looking at my logbook entry, I read "*Hispania* of the East", the *Hispania* being a very scenic, intact wreck lying in the Sound of Mull and famous for its soft corals. Finning forward, superstructure is found rising out of the deck. White toilet bowls shine brightly in the torchlight as do the brass portholes that once let daylight into the washrooms. Further forward, the raised forecastle comes into view, stairs leading up to it on both the port and starboard sides. On the foredeck itself is a massive anchor winch, whose chains can be seen running out through the hawse pipes. Here, misled by what I had read in reports, I dropped over the hull, hoping to see the huge brass eagle. It dawned on me soon enough, when I could find neither rudder nor prop, that I was in fact at the bow. The detour underneath the bow was well worthwhile, though, as the marine life was amazing, with large anemones and the largest grey nudibranchs I have ever seen. I rose up to the port side of the hull and finned along the length of the wreck, passing the winches and portholes. Soon, as the hull started to curve down to the stern, I noted the damage caused in the collision that had sunk her. I was now back at 46 metres and my stops were over 45 minutes. For mid-February in the Firth of Forth, this was a little daunting. Thankfully, though, I had thought to double up on my thermal layers and everything apart from my hands stayed warm through the stops.

Diver inspects bow of German Light Cruiser

Dive no. 14

Name
SMS München

Location
4 miles north of Fidra
GPS coordinates N5607.30
W0246.36

Depth
47–58 metres

Conditions
Visibility is variable, 5–10
metres

Access
Boat only

Diver experience
Advanced/technical diver

Dive site

The *München* is another of the Firth of Forth's most impressive historic wrecks. She was a German pre-Dreadnought light cruiser. Only Scapa Flow in Orkney has the remains of similar ships but, unlike the ones resting there, the *München* played a very active and interesting part in the action at the Battle of Jutland.

Admiral von Reuter was in overall command of the German High Seas Fleet interned in Scapa Flow. At the Battle of Jutland, he was in charge, in the light cruiser *Stettin*, of the 4th Scouting Group. The *München* was second in line in this group, under the command of Commander Oscar Böcker. The boat and the crew were to be very heavily involved in the action. All the ships of the 4th Scouting Group were slow and, by 1916 standards, weakly armed. The *München* could steam at a maximum speed of 22 knots, her armament consisted of ten 4.1-inch guns, two machine guns and two submerged 17.7-inch torpedo tubes and no belt armour and she displaced 3250 tons. Her deck armour was two inches thick apart from at the deck ends which were only ¾ of an inch thick. The conning tower armour was four inches thick, although during the battle even this would be found to be insufficient.

HMS *Falmouth* of the 3rd Light Cruiser Squadron sighted the German ships of the 2nd and 4th Scouting Groups at 2010 hrs on 31 May 1916. The German vessels were oblivious to the presence of British ships until seven minutes later. The ships of the 2nd Scouting Group immediately turned away, eventually drawing fire from British battle cruisers. The 4th Scouting Group, of which the *München* was part, steered a course to intercept the British craft. Battle commenced at 2018 hrs. Two 6-inch shells hit the *München*, the second of which exploded in the upper part of the third funnel. This severely damaged the casings and pipes around the four after-boilers. Even though steam pressure could be maintained only with difficulty, the *München*, along with the *Stettin*, pressed home the attack. The *München* fired 63 shells in this encounter with her enemy but recorded no hits and, at 2031 hrs, the 4th Scouting Group turned away and was quickly lost in the mist. The battle cruiser conflict between the two great naval forces of the age would now begin.

The *München*'s next conflict would erupt out of the darkness at 2235 hrs. The 4th Scouting Group was forced to slow down as two of the German battle cruisers, *Moltke* and *Seydlitz*, crossed the bows of the light cruisers. Ships to the rear of the line, however, were unaware of the reduction in speed and the ships of the 4th Scouting Group closed up in an irregular formation. It was now, at a range of around 3000 yards, that the British 2nd Light Cruiser squadron sighted the German ships. The next three-and-a-half minutes would see a very violent naval exchange and the *München* would expend ninety-two 4.1-inch shells in this short time.

HMS *Southampton* trained her searchlights on the enemy ships and opened fire. The *München*, *Stettin* and *Rostock* exchanged fire with her, shells raining down on the British vessel. Her searchlights were soon destroyed and her guns fell silent. Three cordite fires raged and were nearing the ammunition passage when extinguished. HMS *Southampton* would otherwise have lit the night sky before sinking to the bottom. The Royal Navy vessels in this encounter were certainly beaten in the gunnery battle. The *Southampton*, despite her stricken state, loosed a high-speed torpedo which hit and quickly sank the ancient light cruiser *Frauenlob*, recently dived by the wreck-hunter Innes McCartney. In the chaos, the *München* had to make violent manoeuvres to avoid colliding with the stricken vessel, managing as she did so to fire a torpedo at HMS *Southampton*, but missed her target. The *München* received her punishment and was hit by three 6-inch shells. Two burst in the water near the ship, peppering her hull in 16 places and sending a splinter through the 4-inch armour of the conning tower. The third shell passed through the second funnel and exploded, destroying the starboard rangefinder. For the next two hours, until repairs to a bent wheel shaft could be made, the *München* was steered from the steering gear compartment, as the drive gear in the conning tower had been damaged. After a brief engagement with British destroyers *G11, V1* and *V3* at around 0020 hrs, the *München*'s battle was over apart from firing at imaginary submarines and evading equally imaginary torpedoes. The final threat to the *München* came from her own side. The *Hannover* and *Hessen* opened up on what they thought was a submarine and their violent shooting came very close to causing fatal damage to both the *Stettin* and *München*. Admiral Scheer himself gave the order to cease fire.

The *München* had survived the battle. but eight of her crew had not and a further 20 had been injured. In the end the *München* had fired 161 4.1-inch shells and received five hits from the larger calibre 6-inch guns of the British light cruisers. It's amazing that this very lightly-armed cruiser made it through the battle at all, when every adversary she had faced had been better armed and had had more armour protection.

The war was almost over for the *München* by 18 October 1916, when Admiral Scheer was planning another sortie to confront part of the Grand Fleet. This mission was cancelled, though, the Admiral fearing a trap, when the *München* was torpedoed by a British submarine a few hours after the High Seas Fleet had left the safety of the River Jade, where a German naval base had offered protection from British warships. The *München* did not sink and was offered to the British after the war as part of war reparation, going on to be used for torpedo testing in the Firth of Forth. I do not know if the fatal blow came from an aircraft, a surface vessel or a submarine but it was almost as if the *München*, after all her battles, had given up. As the torpedo struck, she sank very quickly without the need for a second hit.

My dive to the *München* came after a hard day's work. I headed the 20 miles down the coast from Edinburgh to North Berwick, having been fretting all day, fearing that the weather would deteriorate. As I arrived at the harbour, the club RIB was already in the water and the conditions looked ideal. After 15 years of thinking about diving this wreck, it looked very likely that I was at last about to.

The journey out was fast but I noted that the troughs were deepening as we pulled further away from land. The *München* lies 4 miles off the Isle of Fidra as shown on the Admiralty chart. We would be diving on air with a nitrox 50% mix for deco, so needed to dive this wreck on a low neap tide, allowing us to reach the side of the hull at a depth of 48 metres as opposed to well over 50 metres. Going down the shotline, I could hardly wait. The visibility was good and green light followed us down a long way before the water turned a clear black. At 45 metres, my torch beam picked out the starboard side of the *München*, completely encrusted in a carpet of large orange-and-white plumose anemones. As this was our first dive on the wreck, we did not know exactly how she rested on the seafloor. Dropping down the vertical deck, we came to a superstructure which would turn out to be the bridge itself. On top of this was found the ship's wheel, completely encrusted in anemones and marine growth. I can remember thinking that it looked smaller than I expected and had perhaps been thinking of finding a wheel as large as those on old sailing ships. We moved left, which seemed to be the most interesting direction, coming eventually to the bow. On the way, we passed air vents, mooring bollards and anchor hawse pipes with the anchor chains running out from them. I noted a lot of interesting items below deck level, especially where the forward 4.1-inch deck gun turret was once sited. The turret, along with all her armament, was removed prior to her sinking and all that now remains is a large hole in the teak deck. Looking down a deck level, pipes can be seen running along the length of the ship, confirming that these early light cruisers were designed for raiding attacks rather than for lengthy campaigns at sea. This ship had no fewer than ten boilers below deck, along with the two Parsons engines, a normal load of coal, which would amount to 400 tons, and ammunition stores. Space below decks must have been very limited. I felt that to enter the wreck below decks at this depth would be madness, even if interesting brass items did shine below me in my torchlight.

I was amazed that such a deep wreck should be so completely encrusted with soft corals, suggesting that the tide runs fast and hard over it. The *München* really does make a stunning sight. We eventually reached the bow and this forward-sloping structure made an impressive sight, the clean, straight edge of the bow, fringed only by large plumose anemones, sloping down into the darkness. I would have liked to explore this area further but we had planned to stay above 50 metres. This we managed and from the bow we followed the starboard rail, taking in the immensity of the vessel until we arrived back at the shotline where we undertook our 45 minutes of deco stops. After 15 years of waiting to dive this wreck, I had certainly not been disappointed. Delving later into this ship's history only added to the diving experience, for this is a truly special ship, one of the most active in the Battle of Jutland. I felt great respect for the men of both nations who took to the seas in these very lightly-armed ships, understanding, as they must have done, the very real threat of an encounter with an enemy vessel.

Dive no. 15

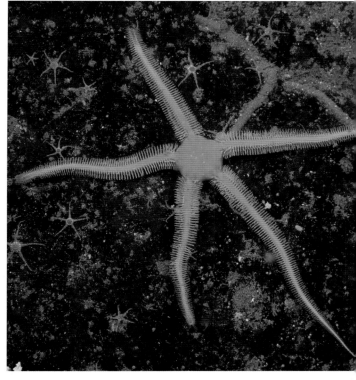

Fidra brittle star

Name
North Dog, Isle of Fidra

Location
3 km west of North Berwick

Depth
15 metres

Conditions
Tide here can run at 3 knots.
Average visibility 4 metres

Access
Boat only

Diver experience
Ocean diver

Dive site
The tide was running hard around the North Dog, a small islet off the northwest side of the Isle of Fidra. With these

conditions I expected a superb dive, but was set to be disappointed. Descending, life is sparse as the tide whips the diver along for 100 metres or so before slackening off. I found this surprising, expecting life to flourish in the tidal water. Where the tide stopped, beds of brittle stars, including yellow specimens, littered the seafloor. Although marine life in general was lacking, we did see an angler fish, which was a real bonus, turning a bland and mundane dive into something a bit special. These fish are said to be seen common here and although nobody can guarantee that interesting fish life will be on station, I would say it's certainly a good site for a second or third dive of the day. There is a prominent archway on the north side of Fidra but it provides less than dynamic diving. All this is not to say that the island should be passed over, although Fidra tends to be overlooked as divers rush to get to the Bass Rock, the area's premier site. Try a different site and you may get lucky.

This island's best potential is as a training site with general depths of 6–8 metres. Underwater photographers will also enjoy this shallow dive. The inner Sound of Fidra is said to make an exhilarating drift dive, but that is one I have yet to do.

Lamb Island short spined scorpion fish

Dive no. 16

Name
Lamb Island

Location
One and a half miles northwest of North Berwick harbour

Depth
8–20 metres

Conditions
Nice easy boat diving. Tide funnels through gullies. Average visibility 6 metres

Access
Boat only

Diver experience
Ocean diver in sheltered areas, sports diver in tidal areas

Dive site
Lamb is shaped like a hog's back and has a sand bar on the shoreward side which joins another

small island. On a sunny day it is very scenic. The diving is at its best on the seaward side of the island, where many of the islets just off Lamb form channels in which the tide sometimes boils through. This is especially true of the northwest corner of the island. The offshore side is a fantastic place for photography. A small cliff drops to around 8 metres before a boulder slope drops to around 20 metres. The slope is clean and free of mud and on a summer's afternoon, in clear visibility, this makes for a dazzling sight. The boulder slope is covered in vivid orange-and-white dead man's fingers. Lobster and edible crabs are common here, but the most impressive residents are the angler fish which are frequently spotted here, especially, of course, when you have left your camera behind. A flat sandy seafloor lies at the base of the boulder slope and the clean golden sand stretches away as far as the limits of the visibility. These sand flats are home to all the burrowing animals as well as flounders and, more rarely, plaice. Run your fingers through the sand and you will be amazed how many dragonets, gobies and prawns dart out in front of you. At the top of the cliff, gullies can be explored in the shallow water, one of them containing large amounts of coal, suggesting a wreck nearby. I have always favoured diving the offshore side of this island or either of its ends, where interesting gullies can be found. There is another dive along the inshore side of the island, which appears to take place on a high ebb tide over the sandbar which connects the island to a small islet, before following the inshore side of the island as a drift dive.

Lion's mane jellyfish

Dive no. 17

Name
Craigleith Island

Location
One mile directly off North Berwick harbour

Depth
12–30 metres

Conditions
Walls to 25 metres and boulder slopes. Average visibility 7 metres

Access
Boat only

Diver experience
Ocean diver

Dive site

Craigleith is the second largest in a chain of islands that lies off North Berwick, and is one mile directly offshore from the town's harbour. This is an excellent dive in its own right, but is usually dived when conditions are marginal and the run to the area's premier dive site, the Bass Rock, is ruled out. Craigleith has cliffs towards its eastern end and the island slopes towards the sea as you travel west. The deepest diving is found around the most easterly-facing cliffs, where, underwater, the cliffs fall away in a series of ledges to over 25 metres. The life here is amazing. Common seals can be found and you may be lucky enough to catch a fleeting glimpse of them underwater. Grey seals are found here too and they are more likely to be encountered by the diver. Cormorant and shag feed here and it is not unusual to find one swimming through your bubbles at 20 metres. Fishlife is better here than at the Bass Rock and colonies of ballan wrasse are found around the shallow boulders and reefs. The encrusting life is good but in no way compares to the northeast face of the Bass Rock. In late summer, large numbers of lion's mane jellyfish arrive here, some as large as dustbins, with trailing, stinging tentacles over 10 metres long. I have never seen these creatures grown to such a large size apart from here, on the east side of Craigleith Island.

The sheltered south face of Craigleith drops to the seafloor, which is 12–15 metres deep, by means of a boulder slope. These boulders form small holes and caves and large fish such as cod and wolffish are frequently spotted. The seafloor, made up of coarse sand and home to flounders, gobies and prawns, is certainly worthy of exploration.

The western end of the island supports similar diving but the sites tend to be shallower and there are slopes rather than cliffs upon which to dive, reflecting the topography of the island itself. The northern face of the island also provides good diving, as this site is more exposed to the elements, but for the best diving at Craigleith, the eastern side is where you want to head.

A Bass Rock gannet

Dive no. 18

Name
Bass Rock

Location
3 miles northeast of North Berwick

Depth
0–50 metres

Conditions

Fantastic scenic diving. Be aware of tidal movement along north face of rock.
Average visibility 8 metres

Access

Boat only

Diver experience

Sports diver, dive leader

Dive site

On rounding the harbour point, the Bass Rock comes into full view. Although it is only one mile directly offshore from the magnificent ruins of Tantallon Castle, it is 3 miles from North Berwick. As you approach, the huge basalt cliffs rise straight out of the sea for over 100 metres. This island has a long and colourful history. St Baldred sought sanctuary here in the eighth century and, much later, a Jacobite garrison held the island's castle for three years, from 1691 to 1694, for King James II and VII against the forces of King William III. In 1920, a lighthouse was built on the remains of this castle and is still in use today. Nowadays, the Bass is best known for its fantastic colony of gannets, here in such large numbers that their plumage and their lime turn the cliffs–and sometimes visiting divers – white. It is a fantastic sight to see them diving in large numbers into the sea to catch fish.

The Bass Rock is basically circular in shape and every heading of the compass provides a different type of diving. The north-facing walls all provide the best diving. The depth increases from around 20 metres to 48 metres as you move along the wall from the northwest to the northeast. The northeast face provides an amazing cliff face which is certainly the best in southeast Scotland. While still on the surface, approaching by boat, keep an eye out for a large flat triangular face on the cliff. Here, underwater, the cliff falls sheer to 46 metres. It is a wise idea to ascertain which way the tide is running and enter the water up-tide. This is especially true if the tide is running to the east, as the cliff is situated near the northernmost point of the Bass and a strong tide can push you off the cliff. I usually enter the water slightly to the west of the main cliff, where the wall still falls sheer to over 30 metres and you can basically pick your depth. The life here is exceptional and, as the walls plummet, the kelp bed is left behind at 6 metres. Huge dahlia anemones of every colour decorate the cliff. Walls of vivid orange-and-white dead man's fingers are so densely packed that they make strobe positioning for macro photography difficult. Large sunstars can be seen and many pink shrimp are to be found in all the nooks and crannies, alongside gobies and squat lobsters. Lobsters and edible crab are common and I wonder, as I look at them, how they can be found on a narrow ledge, halfway up a cliff, in almost 50 metres of water? They must be great climbers. The visibility on average is around 8 metres but can occasionally be as much as 15 metres. At a site like this, that abuts such deep water, you cannot help but wonder if any larger creatures are near at hand. You will usually see small schools of pollack swimming along the cliff, although I must admit I would have expected to see much more fishlife, especially given the amount required to support the colony of gannets and the resident seals. Every so often a porbeagle shark is landed at Dunbar harbour, five miles away, and while it is sad that the shark has been killed, it is good to know that there are some around in the area. I would think that the area probably offers no better place to spot one than here, on the northeast face of the Bass Rock, although it must still be a thousand-to-one chance.

The easternmost face of the Bass Rock forms a cliff to about 25 metres, where small caves and cracks are formed and where wolffish can be found. The seafloor is cut by a series of gullies, with walls around 3 metres high. Life here is less impressive and the sea floor is covered in brittle stars and solitary large anemones. This is a better site for a second dive.

The south face is the most sheltered, at around 8–12 metres deep. The cliff falls onto a sandy seafloor and because it is fairly barren, the site is not often dived by local divers, meaning that there are still potential surprises to be had. The west face supplies similar diving but there are nice caves there. See the next entry (dive site 19, Bass Rock Cave) for further details.

Dive no. 19

Bass Rock cave (entrance to right of lighthouse)

Name
Bass Rock cave

Location
Easternmost entrance, just to right of lighthouse

Depth
Above surface

Conditions
Slippery wet rocks, care must be taken

Access
Access from east or west cave entrance. The east entrance is probably better for cave exploration. Permission is required to land on the Bass Rock and can be obtained from the Scottish Seabird Centre on 01620-890202 (permission is not required for diving activities)

Diver experience
Ocean diver

Dive site
The Bass Rock is the largest single-island breeding colony of North Atlantic gannets in the world. Because of this, landing on the island is sometimes restricted and permission must be sought (see above). If you are permitted to land, you will have many options to fill your surface interval between dives at the Bass Rock. Underneath the lighthouse is a landing point where you can investigate the remains of the old castle. You can then try your hand at completing 'Ye-Haas', jumping from the ten-metre high ledges found around the cliffs to the right of the landing near the cave entrance, but do take care. You can also explore the cave which cuts straight through the Bass Rock for around 120 metres. The easternmost cave entrance is just to the right of the lighthouse and is the most obvious entrance point. The cave entrance here enables you to take a small boat into the cave mouth and makes getting ashore a bit easier, especially if you don't want to get wet. Being above water, it is a dry cave, but the force of the sea is evident in the remains of dead sea birds and seals, washed in on stormy seas. Take a torch to help you walk through the cave, which has large caverns inside, where the rocks are covered in slippery green slime. On nearing the westernmost end of the cave, you may well hear the seals before you see them. At this point it is best if you turn off your torch so as not to spook them. It is also better at this stage not to approach too closely, as they are wild animals and should be respected. You should now see them in the light which comes in from the west cave entrance, where they like to lie on the small pebble beach. If you would like to snorkel with these resident grey seals, bring your boat around to the westernmost cave entrance by passing the lighthouse, as this is the shortest route.

Working out where you think the cave will emerge should lead you right to the western cave entrance. Quietly snorkel up to the pebble beach: it is an impressive sight to see a dozen or so grey seals lying dozing on a beach only metres away. Quite often a youngster will notice you, and immediately the small cave entrance will be filled with seals splashing past. It is fantastic to watch their antics as they demonstrate their skills in the water. In October and November, the grey seal females give birth to their pups and at this time you should avoid disturbing the seals at all. The cave walk and the seal snorkel make for an interesting and exciting interlude before even more exciting encounters beneath the waves at the Bass Rock.

Mike completing deco stops on **Royal Fusilier**

Dive no. 20

Name
Royal Fusilier

Location
4 km northeast of the Bass
Rock
GPS coordinates N5606.39
W0235.36

Depth
42–46 metres

Conditions
Deep wreck. Visibility 5–10
metres

Access
Boat only

Diver experience
Advanced diver/technical diver

Dive site

The *Royal Fusilier* was built in 1924 by Caledon of Dundee and this 2187-ton, 90-metre long ship made the final leg of her last ever journey on 3 June 1941 in the Firth of Forth, steaming to her registered port of Leith. Sailing from London with a general cargo, she was attacked by German Heinkel JU-88 bombers. She started taking on water and was taken under tow but the damage had been done and the ship developed a serious list, sinking 4 kilometres northeast of the Bass Rock off North Berwick. Thankfully, her crew of twenty seven were all saved. What remains on the seafloor is an intact wreck lying on its port side. Although it is completely embedded in the sea floor up to around the centre line of the ship, this wreck has a lot to offer. It lies in 42– 46 metres of water which is swept by tides, so it is definitely a dive for the experienced only. Once you have managed to reach the site, the descent down the shotline can be filled with anticipation. Visibility can vary. If you are lucky you may experience 10 metre visibility and a green tinge to the water, but it is usually dark with visibility around the 5-metre point. Landing on the wreck, you immediately notice that it is covered in life, orange-and-white plumose anemones covering the structures, even at this depth. The first priority is to orientate yourself on the wreck. If you have ever dived the light cruisers in Scapa Flow, you will know that if you land on the hull of the wreck, you need to swim up the hull and drop over the side to find yourself on the deck, now lying vertically in the water. At the stern of this wreck, only three metres of deck protrude from the seafloor, which is at 46 metres. There is a lot of superstructure here, including the remains of a derrick crane. Finning forward along the seafloor, you soon come to a companionway which runs along the starboard side of the ship. Doors lead off from here into the ship, but to enter at this depth is asking for trouble, especially as part of the companionway has a trawl net draped over it. Re-emerging from the companionway, you will notice a lot of debris on the seafloor along with thousands of burrows which house Dublin Bay prawns. Life is also in evidence on the wreck. What appear to be columns that run vertically across the deck are in fact, an illusion: they are ropes hanging down the deck, now covered in plumose anemones. These swell the diameter of the ropes to that of a large tree trunk. Yarrel's blennies scuttle about the anemones and the odd large pollack lurks.

At this point, the diver is just aft of the bridge area and this structure juts out from the deck with a smaller, raised bridge on top of this. This is certainly an area worth further investigation, as this part of the wreck looks as if it has been damaged, quite possibly when the ship sank or when it hit the bottom. Finning further forward towards the bow, the hull sweeps down from the side of the bridge in a large curve to the lower deck level. Here you will pass another large crane and the remains of the mast, lying along the sea floor. Now the side of the hull rises up as it forms the raised shelter at the bow. Here a winch and bollards can be seen. As the bow curves round, it sinks into the mud before the very prow of the ship can be seen. All this exploration will take about 12 minutes and, at this depth, it will perhaps be time to think about returning to the shotline. For this, I find it offers a good opportunity to rise up to the side of the hull and fin back towards the stern. You will pass over intact railings covered in vivid marine life and come to one of the most impressive features of the wreck: parallel lines of large brass portholes, their glass intact, line the hull as far as the eye can see. For someone like myself, who has very rarely seen an intact porthole on any wreck, this is an awesome sight. On reaching one part of the hull which is damaged, lying directly beside one of these large portholes, take a look inside to see, quite clearly in front of you, one of the locking nuts which secure the inner cover. Try to turn the nut and see if, after all this time underwater, it can still turn. It certainly did the last time I tried. Swimming further aft you will pass over more anemone-infested railings and soon you will near the stern area again. Here, as already mentioned, there is a large crane and the sterncastle can also be seen. At this point you have completed the tour of the wreck and will be back at the shotline. It takes about 18 minutes on the wreck to complete the return trip to the stern. This is a superb wreck dive and while you are decompressing, keep an eye out for comb jellyfish and their larger relatives, the lion's mane jellyfish, which can be common above this wreck.

The *Royal Fusilier*'s sister ship *Royal Archer* is also a wreck in the Firth of Forth (see dive site 10).

Dive no. 21

Seacliffe beach submarine pen

Name
Seacliff Harbour Reef (submarine pen)

Location
Point of rock at west end of Seacliff Beach, one mile east of North Berwick. Access from coast road

Depth
8 metres

Conditions
Easy shore dive, ideal training site. Average visibility 6 metres

Access
Park in upper car park, the first one you come to on entering Seacliff Beach (£2 access fee at barrier). Walk 200 metres down to beach and turn left. Access via large gully or submarine pen

Diver experience
Ocean diver

Dive site
Seacliff Beach is located one mile east of North Berwick. Just after you pass the impressive remains of Tantallon Castle, there is a sharp right-hand bend. Drive straight on here, along the farm track that leads to the beach. Parking at the upper car park seriously reduces the length of walk you have to undertake to reach the site. Once onto

Seacliff Beach, head over to the red sandstone point on your left. A large, obvious gully will open up at the base of an isolated sandstone mound. This is the entry point for the dive. If the tide is high, you have an alternate entry point. A very small harbour is to be found here, referred to, for some reason, as the Sub Pen, although it's so small that that even the Midget X-craft described in dive site 11 would not fit into it. Today the little harbour is used by a creel boat, so please be aware of this if you wish to undertake jump entries from the harbour walls. The dive itself is fantastic as a training site and as a general guddle. Keep the reef wall on your right-hand side and follow it around the point. There are nice little walls and gullies to explore with nudibranchs, spider crabs and sea urchins. Lobsters and edible crabs are plentiful as well, and the sandy seafloor is home to large numbers of small flatfish. Holes and crevices in the rocky reef are full of encrusting life and the odd large cod hides in here as well. For the novice diver this will be an exciting dive with a lot to see and it is also a worthwhile site for the macro- photographer. On rounding the point you will exit onto the fantastic beach at Seacliff with the red ruins of Tantallon Castle in the background. Keep a look out for seal pups playing in the surf as there are a couple of seal colonies nearby and sightings are frequent. The magnificent dive site at the Bass Rock is one mile directly offshore from the beach, letting the trainee divers know that there are even more exciting dives to experience once their training is completed.

Lobster at St Baldred's boat

Dive no. 22

Name
St Baldred's Boat

Location
Rocky point at east end of Seacliff. Large memorial cross at site

Depth
10 metres

Conditions
Superb shallow dive. Surprisingly fierce tides. Average visibility 6 metres

Access
Boat dive recommended. Can be dived from shore but long walk and strong tides

Diver experience
Ocean diver/sports diver

Dive site
To shore dive this site, park at the lower car park at Seacliff Beach. From there, it's around 400 metres to the end of the reef. Walking out over the reef is not advisable as it is bisected by deep gullies that cannot be stepped across. I have made this mistake here and clambering across reef gullies that are high and dry is no fun at all. Please take my word for it that it is best to undertake this site only at high tide, when snorkelling out is an option.

This site is well worth the considerable effort that is required to dive here. Once in 6–8 metres of water, descend and head out toward the cross at the end of the point. Always be aware of the tide at this site as the shallow water and gullies make for a lot of water movement. If you find conditions difficult because of the tide do not attempt to round the point. This little dive site looks very beautiful and benign above the surface but down below, the tide fairly rips around, which is why the marine life is so good. It's also the reason why I recommend that you only undertake this dive by boat! Underwater here the wall falls to around 6–10 metres and the rocks are full of cracks and crevices. These are all full of lobster which cannot withdraw out of sight because the cracks are too shallow to accommodate them. This generally leads to lobsters flapping about backwards in the open water and it's great fun watching them trying to evade the diver. I even had one caught up between the medium-pressure hoses of my regulator. The difficulty of diving this site means, I hope, that a lot of these lobsters have been able to survive to a grand old age. Grey seals also live on the point and are often seen on the surface. If you are lucky, you may have a furry friend following you around on your dive. As well as the entertaining marine life, there is wreckage at this site, mainly flattened plates but also a large anchor.

This little site is a real delight and holds many surprises for the diver. Take care with the tide and you will easily fill an hour at this fantastic, under-dived site.

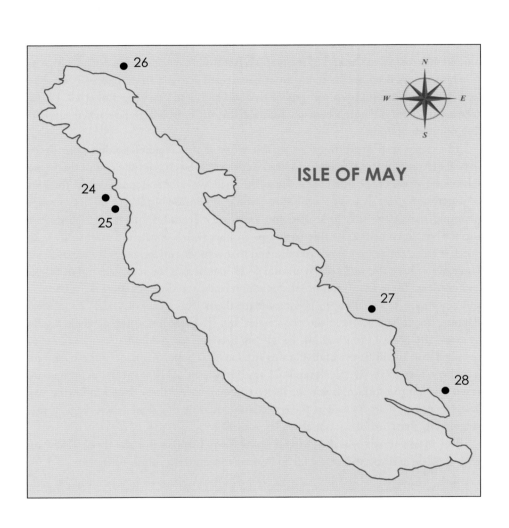

ISLE OF MAY

The Isle of May is a long island, its eastern face low-lying but with high cliffs rising out of the sea on its western edge The island is a National Nature Reserve, a haven for birds and marine life and an important breeding colony for grey seals, puffins, guillemots and razorbills. There is a small ranger station near the east landing which is worth a visit if you are lucky enough to land on the island between dives. It is full of information about the island's historical sites and the creatures you will find here.

The diving around the Isle of May is generally scenic diving. The island has been, however, the grave of many a ship and there are a number of broken wrecks around its coastline. Further offshore, some spectacular deeper wrecks can be found, including the magnificent K-boats that were involved in the Battle of May Island.

To reach the island, you can launch boats from North Berwick and Dunbar but the closest slipway to the island is found on the Fife coast at Anstruther, where there is a good launch point. The island lies 5 miles from Anstruther, 13 miles from North Berwick and 10 miles from Dunbar.

The island is regularly visited by Marine Quest, The Dive Bunker, Aquatrek and Forth Diving Services.

Grey Seal, May Island

Dive no. 23

Divers exploring stern of Primrose *wreck*

Name
Primrose

Location
Half a mile southwest of the
Isle of May
GPS coordinates N5610.69
W0233.44

Depth
30–32 metres

Conditions
Very nice scenic wreck. Strong
tides, slack water required.
Visibility 5–10 metres

Access
Boat only

Diver experience
Dive leader

Dive site
As the *Primrose* sank half a mile
southwest of the Isle of May, she
lies in 32 metres of water, slightly deeper than the other wrecks
associated with the island. She
was a Peterhead fishing trawler
that ran onto the rocks in 1904.
Salvage attempts failed and the *Primrose* slipped beneath the waves for us divers to
enjoy. Visibility at this site can be variable but it is often over 10 metres. Descending
down the shotline in good visibility, the diver will be able to see the shape of the hull
in the sandy seafloor. Nothing much of the hull protrudes above the sand now, apart
from at the bow and stern. At the bow there are mooring bollards on each side of the
prow and a large A-frame structure. By this time your eyes will be getting used to the
darkness at this depth and the water takes on a blue hue. Orange-and-white dead man's
fingers can be seen covering a large structure in the distance. Finning aft, this turns
out to be a large single boiler, its exterior covered by soft corals and big pollack gliding
around it. Exploring the boiler, the diver will find little Yarrel's blennies inhabiting the
small pipes on its face, in which small lobsters sometimes hide as well. Make sure you
look under the plates and pipes on the seafloor as there is a good chance that you will

come across a large ling or conger eel, hoping to avoid detection. Moving further aft, the engine block has a similar covering of anemones and is home to some ballan wrasse. Near here, on the seafloor, are the remains of a bathroom. Black-and-white tiles can be seen on the floor and there is a large upturned sink lying against the superstructure. Aft of this, broken plates and the keel of the ship lead you back towards the stern. The rudder and propeller are both still visible and the stem of the keel rises 2 metres up off the seabed. Another set of mooring bollards can be seen here. You have now covered the length of the *Primrose*. If you have the required gas and time in hand, you may wish to spend some more time exploring the boiler and the engine block as you make your way back to the shotline, perhaps following the other side of the wreck. Soon, though, the tide will start to tug and it will be time to be back up the shotline, reflecting on your dive on one of the Isle of May's most popular wrecks.

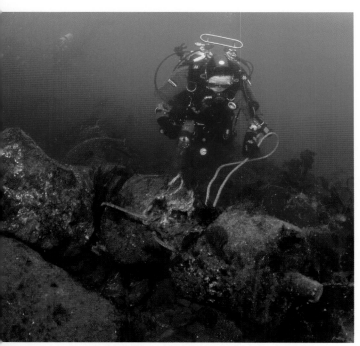

Exploring the Anlaby

Dive no. 24

Name
Anlaby

Location
In Altarstanes Bay, just south of the west landing of the Isle of May
GPS coordinates N5611.30 W0233.88

Depth
8–18 metres

Conditions
Easy wreck dive. Average visibility 8 metres

Access
Boat only

Diver experience
Ocean diver

Dive site

In 1873, the steamship *Anlaby* did not travel far on her last journey from Granton, a port lying to the west of Leith Docks. It was only around 20 miles, in thick fog, before she ran straight onto the Isle of May and became a total loss.

Any diver who has been lucky enough to dive at the Isle of May will know of the *Anlaby*. The wreck is easy to locate and lies at a shallow depth, so is ideal for the second or third dive of the day. The wreck lies bow-into-shore and ribs and spars start to form in 8 metres. The best way to find it is to fin down the rocky reef to the 12–14 metre contour and fin south at this depth, which should bring you onto the wreck. In truth, there is not much left of *Anlaby* but the spars, keel and broken plates are home to a lot of marine life. Bright orange cushion stars are found on the ribs and spars, and gangs of large pollack cruise around. Families of ballan wrasse have made the wreck their home and they will give you a close inspection. There are lots of small pipefish and crabs in the kelp and weed that cover the shallower areas of the wreck. As you move deeper there is more wreckage. The stern is the most impressive area, where you will be able to see the large four-bladed propeller and the rudder. There is also a winch and some anchor chain lying on the seabed here. This wreck is a real thrill for novice divers and photographers who will easily enjoy an hour here. For most other divers, though, a once-over will be enough before options such as moving onto the sand to look for scallops or following the reef towards the south (see dive site 25) become very attractive. If you have never dived the *Anlaby*, don't let this put you off, though, as there is a lot to see at this site.

The west landing on the Isle of May is also a popular spot for conducting 'Ye-Haas'. It's great fun but do check the depth first.

Dive no. 25

Name
Wall dive south of west landing, Altarstanes Bay, Isle of May

Location
South of the wreck of the *Anlaby* (dive site 24).
200 metres south of west landing at cliff
GPS coordinates N5611.30 W0233.88

Depth
10–15 metres

Conditions
Shallow wall with lots of interesting life. Average visibility 6 metres

Access
Boat only

Ballan wrasse and reef at Anlaby *wall dive*

Diver experience
Ocean diver

Dive site
I found this site by chance after drifting off the wreck of the *Anlaby*. Fin south from the wreck and pick up the wall. When you reach this site the marine life instantly becomes more colourful, with the usual orange-and-white dead man's fingers covering the walls. You will also see a lot of fish here, notably very large pollack. There will also be cod hiding under the boulders on the seafloor and friendly families of ballan wrasse will come close to have a look at you, although they may not be quite as tame as their relatives down in St Abbs. Small gullies, just waiting to be explored, open up as you drift along in the shallow water. Depending on the time of year, you may be lucky and have a fantastic experience when diving this site. As the Isle of May is a considerable distance offshore, migratory birds that move offshore to feed can still be found here in large numbers when they have left the mainland. I dived here at the beginning of July one year and as I drifted along the shallow wall with my brother we were buzzed by puffins, guillemots and razorbills. Streaking silver birds swimming around us for a long time made for a fantastic experience. May, June and July are the best months to enjoy the antics of these amazing marine birds.

The cliffs on the west side of the Isle of May are generally very impressive above the surface and there are some extremely nice sites to explore here. Unfortunately, when I have been out here, I have been with parties who concentrated on wreck diving, but I certainly plan to carry on exploring the western cliffs, as they look like spectacular dive sites. This little dive makes for a fantastic way to continue a dive after enjoying the wreck of the *Anlaby* (dive site 24). If you can manage to dive here at the right time of year, your experience of diving with birds will be a memorable one.

Diver on wall of Mars *wreck site*

Dive no. 26

Name
The Mars wreck

Location
Mars Rock, North Ness, Isle of May
GPS coordinates N5611.59
W0234.00

Depth
21–30 metres

Conditions
Kelp-covered cliff face. Average visibility 10 metres

Access
Boat only

Diver experience
Sports diver

Dive site
This site looks very attractive above the water as Mars Rocks are usually covered by their resident colony of grey seals. There is a high probability that you will, at the very least, get a glimpse of a seal underwater here. As for finding the Mars wreck, that is somewhat more difficult. I personally don't believe that much of the wreck survives and what does is covered by thick kelp in shallow gullies. I did not find any significant wreckage at this site and finned out over the nice wall and drifted around in the tide. The wall is smooth and there is not that much life once you leave the shallows. At 20 metres it was fairly bland, with only patches of dead man's fingers, the odd sea urchin and some nice starfish. What are nice, though, are the shoals of small pollack that school along the top of the cliffs below the kelp zone. Rising back up the wall to around 10 metres, the covering of dead man's fingers thickens and pipefish are common in the kelp stalks and weed. Nudibranchs and nice yellow sea lemons can also be seen. If you are really lucky you may have a boisterous grey seal pup wanting to play with you when you surface.

This site may not be the best of dives but is known for its seal encounters. It's probably best regarded as a second dive of the day.

Dive no. 27

Name
Island

Location
Island Rocks, northeast side of
Isle of May
GPS coordinates N5611.15
W0232.95

Depth
18 metres

Conditions
Excellent scenic wreck. Average
visibility 10 metres

Access
Boat only

Diver experience
Ocean diver

Dive site

Angler fish at the Island *wreck*

The *Island* was a grand steamship, used for a time as the Danish Royal Yacht. At just under 1800 tons, she was a fairly big ship and had almost completed her journey from Copenhagen to Leith when, in thick fog, she ran into the Isle of May and never left. Today she makes an interesting site for the diver. I like to start the dive by exploring the large obvious gully just to the north of the wrecksite. This is extremely scenic and patches of dead man's fingers and sea urchins add colour to the walls, The shredded kelp that lies on the bottom of the gully is full of pipefish and crabs. The gully shallows up to only 3 metres deep. Here, lobsters are found in small caves in the wall. For the wreck diver, large sections of brass piping from the *Island* have been washed into this gully and can be seen lying here in the shallows. After spending a short time in the gully it is time to find the remains of the wreck. To do this, fin straight out of the gully to 14 metres and turn right, maintaining this depth. The seabed is a sloping, rocky reef full of hiding places. Wolffish are often found here and also watch out for angler fish: it was here that I saw the largest specimen I have ever seen. Beautiful red sunstars grow to a large size here and their smaller relatives, brittle stars, cling to all the prominent rocks to filter plankton in the tide. After 100 metres or so of finning, you will start to encounter wreckage, mainly flattened plates. You can see where portholes were once fitted to the sheets of rusty steel. Fish are attracted to the wreckage and beautiful red lion's mane jellyfish pulse over it, making a very pretty sight In the green water, especially if the sun is shining. The primary remaining feature of the *Island* is a single large boiler, which you will find by continuing to fin over the wreckage at 14 metres. The *Island* may now be in a flattened state but her remains are covered in marine life, which, along with a trip out to the fantastic Isle of May, will make for a very pleasant experience for the diver.

Dive no. 28

Name
The Pillow

Location
Just north of the entrance to Kirkhaven landing, Isle of May GPS coordinates N5610.99 W0232.93

Depth
5–30 metres

Conditions
Sloping rocky reef. Average visibility 7 metres

Access
By boat

Diver experience
Ocean diver

Dive site
Diving straight out from Kirkhaven, the east landing point on the Isle of May, you will come across the remains of the wreck of the *Scotland*, although this is said to be nothing more than a large boiler. I have never dived at this site, as when

Bright red sunstar at the Pillow

we planned to do so, we were told of wreckage that had been found just to the north of this site, at a place known as the Pillow.

Enter here close to the shore, where the water is 5 metres deep. Finning offshore through some small, fairly barren gullies will bring the diver out onto the reef. This falls away in a moderate slope to over 30 metres. Coarse sand makes up the seafloor and metre-high ledges of rock intermittently rise up through it, forming shallow gullies.

Marine life here is spartan and pockets of orange-and-white dead man's fingers and the odd dahlia anemone can be seen on the exposed reef. The diver will fairly quickly note that there are better areas to dive on the Isle of May. I mention this site, though, as interesting items of wreckage can be found here. Twenty-millimetre cannon shells were most likely fired from an aircraft during the war or, as deposits of the shells were found together, an aircraft may have crashed in the area. A large white object also found here was thought by my buddy possibly to have been the perspex cockpit of a Mosquito aircraft, although from later research, I wondered if it might have been a type of explosive. If you dive this site, be careful what you touch in case the unidentified object is dangerous. If I were to visit this site again, I would opt to dive on the remains of the *Scotland,* as a boiler and wreckage at the more tidal southern end of the Isle of May would be much more exciting than the Pillow, which I found pretty dull. That said, the inquisitive diver who persists in diving this site may be lucky and find some more substantial wreckage, possibly that of an aircraft.

Sneland 1 *diver decompressing*

Dive no. 29

Name
Sneland I

Location
1.5 miles southeast of the Isle of May
GPS coordinates N5609.69 W0230.85

Depth
58 metres maximum. Upper hull side 48 metres

Conditions
Deep intact wreck. Average visibility 15 metres

Access
Boat only

Diver experience
Advanced diver/technical diver

Dive site
Germany was about to sign complete unconditional surrender at midnight on 7 May 1945.

The European conflict would be over and VE Day would dawn. Kapitänleutnant Emil Klusmeier would later claim that he had no knowledge of the order issued by Gross Admiral Karl Dönitz on 4 May. Dönitz had succeeded Hitler and had instructed all U-boats that they were to cease all wartime operations in light of the imminent German surrender. One hour before the surrender declaration was officially signed, a convoy of five merchant ships and their escorts were running out of the Firth of Forth and drawing level with the Isle of May. The night sky then exploded with a ball of fire as two of the merchantmen were torpedoed in quick succession. The *Avondale Park* and the *Sneland I* were the targeted ships in the convoy and they were the last two ships to be sunk in the European theatre of World War Two, the *Avondale Park* being the last British ship sunk in the conflict. They both now lie on the seafloor of the Firth of Forth. I have dived the *Sneland I*, a Norwegian steamship originally named *Ingeborg* when she was launched at Stettin in Germany. It's a long way to drop down a shotline but the visibility is often spectacular at this site. It is not unusual to experience blue-water diving with 20 metres visibility. The stern section of the *Sneland I* lies on her starboard side. Large winches are visible below the diver as they swim over the hull at 48 metres and take in the now-vertical deck. This is a large vessel and the fittings look massive. Below, on the seafloor, the mast now runs horizontally out from the deck. Finning aft towards the stern, the most impressive feature comes into view: a very large gun and turret aimed straight back over the stern. Diving this wreck on air will be pushing the limits of recreational diving as the depth here at the top of the deck is around 53 metres. Air will only enable the diver the briefest of visits, so I would recommend a trimix mix for this dive. Once the stern is reached, the diver can rise up to the railings that still surround it, now covered in orange-and-white plumose anemones. Then, once on top of the hull, the diver can fin back to the shotline, still looking down on the superstructure and passing some massive portholes on the way. The *Sneland I* is an incredibly interesting wreck dive and I certainly look forward to a return visit to explore it further.

THE BATTLE OF MAY ISLAND

On 31 January 1918, forty Royal Navy vessels left the shelter of their base at Rosyth in Fife. It was a misty evening and darkness was falling. Each vessel displayed only a dim stern light, and radio silence was to be strictly enforced.

Lead by the cruisers HMS *Courageous* and HMS *Irthuriel*, the great line of ships stretched out for 30 miles in a single line behind the lead cruiser. At the Isle of May, where the great Firth of Forth opens out, the ships all increased their speed to 20 knots, the K-class subs proving their pedigree by being able to keep up with the main battle fleet at this high speed, with even a few knots in reserve. No other sub could do that.

Two minesweeping trawlers, completely unaware of the massive fleet operation, steamed straight into the line in front of the K-boats. Emergency evasive action ensued and, in turning hard to port, the rudder of *K-14* jammed. The next boat in line, *K-12*, along with the disabled *K-14*, turned on their navigation lights while the rudder was repaired. When the rudder was eventually freed, the subs rejoined the line but *K-14* was hit by the following sub, *K-22*.

Both subs were stopped and *K-14* was sinking. Radio silence was broken and a message sent to the squadron's lead cruiser, stating that the stricken subs could make port. So, with the 2nd Battle Cruiser squadron bearing down upon them at 20 knots, the two subs limped back to port, and straight into the path of HMS *Inflexible*. Ten metres of the bow of *K-22* was bent at right angles in the collision, and she settled with only her conning tower above the waves. It was at this time that the captain of HMS *Irthuriel* was handed the decoded message relating to the earlier collision of *K-22* and *K-14*. He decided to turn about and go to the aid of the damaged boats. So, leading the remaining K-boats behind him, he turned straight into the path of the 2nd Battle Cruiser squadron, which had carried on completely unaware of their collision with *K-22*.

Violent manoeuvres ensued and, miraculously, collisions were avoided, but the Battle of the Isle of May was not finished yet. The curse of the K-class would strike again before the night was out. (*K-22* had originally been named *K-13* but she sank during her sea trials, killing all her crew. She was salvaged and renamed.) HMS *Irthuriel* and her tail of K-boats were nearing the island when out of the murk loomed HMS *Fearless*. *K-17* was directly in the light cruiser's path and was hit, sinking very quickly but with most of her crew making it out. Photographs of HMS *Fearless* would later show that a large area of her bow section had caved in. The K-boats following HMS *Fearless* now had to take evasive action to avoid their flotilla leader. *K-12* narrowly avoided a collision with the battle cruiser HMS *Australia* and, in so doing, headed directly for *K-6*. Disaster then struck as the evasive manoeuvres of *K-6* put her on a collision course with *K-4*. *K-4* was hit and almost cut in two in a massive collision as the two 100-metre long vessels smashed into each other. *K-4* sank immediately, taking her crew with her. No escape was possible, as she was rammed and pushed under by *K-7* as she was sinking.

The surviving crew of *K-17* were still floundering in the water when the 5th Battle Squadron arrived on the scene. Completely unaware of the incident, the three battleships and their destroyer screen mowed through the survivors. Only eight men survived.

In all, over 100 men died that night, two subs were lost and four damaged as was the light cruiser HMS *Fearless*. As this was wartime, the disaster remained a secret. Only as recently as 2002 was a memorial cairn erected to the memory of the brave submariners who lost their lives.

Knowing the history always adds to the experience of diving important wrecks. We took only pictures and left only bubbles on our visit to the site of the disaster and the resting place of the crews of *K-4* and *K-17*.

K-CLASS SUBMARINES

The K-class of British submarine had such a poor safety record that, unofficially, they were named the Killer-, Koffin-, Katastophe- or Kalamity-class. A lot of submariners died in these subs and the K-class boat was generally loathed by the crews. Only one K-boat, *K-7*, engaged an enemy vessel, firing a salvo of torpedoes, one of which scored a direct hit under the conning tower of *U-95* but which failed to explode. This was the curse of the K-class in action.

Strangely, these massive submarines were driven by steam power. As the submarine dived, the funnels would collapse, sealing off the boilers which would be dowsed. Once the boat had dived, electric batteries provided power. These were immense vessels, 1980 tons and 103 metres long. They were designed to travel fast on the surface, at 24 knots, scouting ahead of the Grand Fleet's battleships and cruisers in World War One. Their role, once an enemy had been spotted, was to dive and surface behind the enemy vessels, blocking any escape.

Interestingly, when hostilities ended after World War One, further orders for K-boats were cancelled. Some of the K-boat hulls were partially completed and these became the M-class submarine. These vessels became infamous in their own right: the *M-1*, for being fitted with a 12-inch battleship gun and the *M-2*, fitted with an aircraft hangar – but their history, as they say, is another story.

K4 *toppled conning tower*

Dive no. 30

Name
K-4 (British steam-powered submarine)

Location
Northeast of the Isle of May GPS coordinates unavailable. Contact Marine Quest to arrange dive.

Depth
48–54 metres

Conditions
Often superb. Average visibility 10 metres but can reach 20 metres

Access
Boat only

Diver experience
Advanced diver/technical diver

Dive site

K-4 is a monstrous submarine – these vessels were over 100 metres long – lying intact on the seafloor. Due to their depth, the K-class boats are big dives but if you are qualified, they should not be missed. *K-4* is right up there on my favourite dive site list. Visibility in the summer months is often superb and it is not uncommon to be descending in 20-metre visibility.

As you reach 45 metres, the huge bulk of this immense submarine appears in front of you. Arriving at the midsection of the wreck, the diver will notice that the conning tower has been displaced and lies on the deck, leaning over to the starboard side. Cables can be seen inside the tower while outside, along its top, periscopes protrude. Round brass portholes are visible on the front. Finning forward, the deck is so wide that it feels more like finning along the flight deck of an aircraft carrier than a submarine. Keep a look out for large scorpion fish that nestle in the orange-and-white plumose anemones that cover this wreck. Thick metal hawsers lie outside their stowage lockers as sections of the deck have rotted away. Just forward of this can be seen the anemone-encrusted gun, its barrel pointing directly to the surface. It was the large elevation wheel that alerted me to what I was looking at, as I had not been expecting the gun to be in an elevated position. Forward of this structure, on the deck, are two parallel lines, around one metre apart. Partially buried in a layer of silt are links of anchor chain that run along the grooves before dropping into their hawse pipes. Fifteen metres back from the bow, hydroplanes protrude from the sides of the hull, in the retracted position and looking very small on the wreck. No wonder these vessels were difficult to control. Finning further over this huge foredeck, mooring bollards can be seen, while the anchor, tight in its hawse pipe, is 5 metres back from the bow. Dropping down the port side of the hull, slightly below and forward of the anchor, at a depth of 53 metres, the torpedo tubes are visible. The doors are open and you can see through to the other side of the wreck. The diver is now at the base of the bow which rises straight up five anemone-fringed metres, making a great sight. The diver can now fin along the starboard side of the wreck, taking in all the sights again. Once aft of the coning tower there are other points of interest to investigate. Firstly you will come across the raised superstructure that housed the funnels. On top of this is another deck gun. Massive hatches are open where the funnels would have sat. Further aft there are some strange features which I initially thought were the boilers themselves, but which turned out to be the massive mushroom valves that ventilated the engine room while the submarine was on the surface. As *K-4* lies completely upright on the bottom with a bow-up attitude, the stern of the wreck is partly obscured in the mud and the screws and rudder are not visible. I would suggest that her best features are the bow section back to the gun, aft of the conning tower. If you want to see the screws and investigate the stern section I would suggest diving *K-17* (dive site 31) where the screws are still free of the seafloor.

Dive no. 31

K17 *stern gun and hatch*

Name
K-17 (submarine)

Location
East of the Isle of May
GPS coordinates unavailable. Contact Marine Quest to arrange dive

Depth
49–57 metres

Conditions
Superb wreck dive. Average visibility 10 metres

Access
Boat only

Diver experience
Advanced diver/technical diver

Dive site
K-17 lies less than 100 metres from the remains of K4 (dive site 30). She lies in slightly deeper water with a maximum depth of 57 metres. When *K-17* was sunk in a collision with HMS *Fearless*, the submarine's bow was completely severed and around 15 metres of it are completely missing. The best sites to dive on this wreck are from the conning tower back to the stern of the vessel. The conning tower, which has now fallen from the deck, lies on the seafloor on the starboard side of the wreck. It may sometimes be difficult to see, though, as *K-17* lies at an angle across the tidal flow and is therefore affected much more by the tide than is *K-4*. Aft of the ripped-off conning tower, the diver will arrive at the remains above the engine room. Huge hatches can be seen where once the steam funnels would have opened and closed. Then come four clam-like structures, the mushroom valves that were opened to ventilate the boilers while the submarine travelled on the surface. On *K-17*, one of these is in the open position and the mechanical arm that opened the vent can clearly be seen. The other three are in a partially-opened position, looking like (with apologies to younger readers) the smiling mouths of the potato robots in the 1970s advert for Smash. Aft of the vents there is an unidentifiable structure on the deck, which may be the remains of the funnel mechanism. Aft of this is a very impressive deck gun, whose long barrel, pointing forward, is topped by a muzzle cap. It is completely covered in plumose anemones. This is already amazing diving but the best features are yet to come. Moving aft and dropping down the port side of the submarine to 57 metres, the diver can view the last remaining visible propeller of any K-class boat. Two blades are free from the sand and the pointed boss can clearly be seen. The aft hydroplane on this side has been ripped off. Finning under the stern, the single large rudder can be seen, partially buried. Moving around to the starboard side of the wreck, the propeller here is almost hidden under the sand. Only one blade of the propeller is visible but the starboard hydroplane is intact. The coning tower is now 50 metres in front of you on the seabed, but at this

depth that is a big swim. It is therefore a good idea to ascend nearly 6 metres to the deck and fin forward over its amazing features to find the shotline. Even if the water is clear it can be dark and flashing strobes attached to the shotline are a welcome sight. I wonder if these two magnificent K-boats will ever be connected by a rope and, if they are, who the first diver will be to dive both subs in one go? One thing is certain: that diver will be using a good propulsion device and will have to be prepared to do an amazing amount of decompression. For the average technical diver, exploring one of these submarines at a time will provide all the excitement they need.

The wrecks of these strange submarines are an amazing piece of British history and, once you know the story behind them, provide a memorable dive.

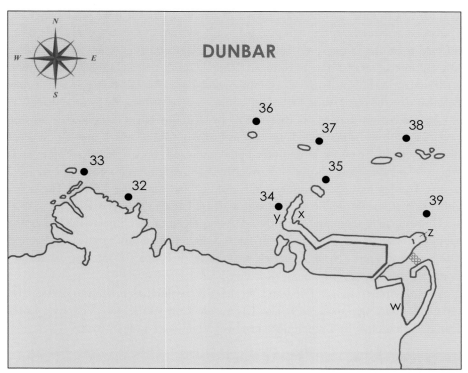

w – slipway
x – entry point for Johnstone's Hole & exit for Harbour Reef & Johnstone's Hole
y – entry point for Harbour Reef
z – Battery Reef and Yetts entry point
○   boulders block access

DUNBAR

Dunbar lies 25 miles east of Edinburgh and is quite a sizeable town with a large red sandstone harbour. Its entrance is guarded by the remains of a once-grand castle, often referred to as one of the seven keys to Scotland. Unfortunately it has recently fallen into an unrecognisable state of disrepair. Happily for us divers, Dunbar's underwater environment is still in first-class condition, and I recommend that you take a look before it gets too busy. At present, most of the sites are visited only by local divers.

An old battery fort at the east end of the harbour offers obvious shore-diving potential, with five small islands in view just offshore, all of which provide excellent diving. Keep an eye on the water in the harbour too and you are likely to see grey seals which follow the fishing boats in. Further offshore, magnificent wrecks are available to dive. Dunbar harbour dries at low tide, making boat launching difficult. Two hours either side of low tide will ensure enough water to launch the largest RIB.

Unfortunately there are currently no diving facilities at Dunbar. The closest air supplies are at North Berwick or St Abbs. Charter boats diving the sites around Dunbar are Marine Quest, Aquatrek, who bring their boats from their bases, and Forth Diving Services. who moor their dive boat at Dunbar.

Dunbar offers a range of bed-and-breakfast accommodation, caravan parks, pubs, restaurants and supermarkets. It also has an excellent leisure pool, and East Links Family Park is close by. Edinburgh is just over 30 minutes away by road.

Dunbar Harbour and Castle

Dive no. 32

Coral
Canyon
Gully

Old Pool
Gully

Bathe Reef, Dunbar, entry points

Name
The Old Pool, Bathe Reef

Location
500 metres west of harbour

Depth
Average depth 12 metres, can reach maximum of 16 metres

Conditions
Easy shore dive once at waterside. Average visibility 5 metres

Access
From Marine Road, Dunbar via steep steps at war memorial

Diver experience
Ocean diver

Dive site
I have to look back a long way through my logbooks before I find an entry for this dive.
I did a lot of my initial training here and went on to train divers at this site. Labelling
the site purely as a good spot for training is, however, a little unfair. The worst thing
about this dive site is the entry or, rather, the exit. Fifty or sixty steep steps have to be
negotiated down – and up – the cliff. So, lame as the excuse might be, I tend to avoid
this site.

Once you have braved the steps and recovered, you will see, directly in front of you,
the Old Pool, a natural area of water which, with the aid of some brickwork, was used

for bathing back in the good old days, giving its name to the reef and the dive site. Wade out into the pool and kit up at its seaward side, where an inviting gully takes you out to the reef. This is a nice point to descend as tall fronds of kelp cover the roof of the gully, making it very scenic. Keep the reef on your left-hand side and follow it round. There are some really nice gullies here with lots of nudibranchs and cowries to be seen. After this, the seafloor flattens out a bit so fin back inshore to pick up the cliff again. If you are lucky, you will note a narrow vertical crack running up the cliff, only wide enough for a single diver to fin through. Once inside, you'll see a large circular blowhole, big enough for two divers to explore at a time, rises right up to the surface. This blowhole is not to be confused with the blowhole described at the Harbour Point (dive site 34). It is full of life with beautiful small white anemones covering parts of the wall and hydroids being fed upon by nudibranchs. Spider crabs walk around the walls and there are always scorpion fish waiting for a snack. There is nothing large in this blowhole, though, as in stormy conditions it is your proverbial washing machine. On rougher days water can be seen shooting out the top, giving away the blowhole's position, just to the right of a large gully that cuts into the reef as you look out to sea. A short walk across the reef top to this point enables you to enter the water here and pick up the blowhole immediately. On exiting the blowhole, and continuing along to the left, the large sheer-sided gully can now be explored. This gully, which is full of life including big lobsters, and the blowhole, are the major features of this dive site. Continuing on the dive, the reef becomes a tangle of kelp across shallow boulders. It's best to skirt around the worst of this by heading into deeper water. The next exciting feature that you will see is Coral Canyon, described in dive site 33. Continuing around, following the reef, you will be able to exit the dive at the large gully at the west end of the reef.

Old Pool scorpion fish

Dive no. 33

Name
Coral Canyon

Location
500 metres west of Dunbar harbour

Depth
16 metres

Conditions
Scenic dive with single gully. Average visibility 5 metres

Access

From Marine Road, Dunbar via steps at war memorial, across The Delves

Diver experience

Ocean diver

Dive site

As with the Old Pool (dive site 32) I have had to look back a long way through my logbooks before finding an entry for this site. The reason is the same: those fifty or sixty steep steps that have to be navigated to make your way up or down the cliff.

Once you have tackled them, though, and have got to the bottom, walk around the base of the cliffs to your left rather than crossing to the Old Pool. You will see a vast red sandstone reef in front of you, known as the Delves. It has to be crossed for around 300 metres to the large, obvious gully at the west end of the reef. This is the exit gully for the Old Pool dive. Even at high tide, the water should only reach your ankles as you cross the Delves. Catch your breath and kit up at the end of the gully and fin out right to the end, ignoring the false gullies that open up, which are very shallow and uninteresting. Keep the reef wall on your right-hand side and fin out along the reef. Soon you will come to a deep hole and the Coral Canyon that drops down into 16 metres. This is around 6 metres deeper than the surrounding terrain, full of soft corals and covered in dead men's fingers. Small blennies and squat lobsters abound and this is a pretty little site. Once you have fully explored the canyon, find the main reef again and either re-trace your fin strokes back to the entrance gully or continue your dive around Bathe Reef, passing the gullies and blowhole to emerge at the Old Pool.

Perhaps I will get a rich nitrox mix and revisit the Old Pool and Coral Canyon, as writing about the sites has rekindled my interest. The nitrox, of course, will be just to help me up those steps.

Dive no. 34

Two-spot goby on Harbour Reef

Name
Harbour Reef

Location
Entrance to Dunbar harbour

Depth
4–12 metres

Conditions
Easy dive, ideal training site. Be aware of proximity to harbour fairway. Average visibility 5 metres

Access
Shore entry 1 metre high, stride entry into water (dependent on tide). Best dived at high tide

Diver experience
Ocean diver

Dive site
Harbour Reef is a slab of rock that juts out into the sea, extending the southern entrance wall of the harbour. This dive is quite shallow, so diving at high tide is recommended. You can circumnavigate the whole headland in about 20 minutes, making it an ideal site for a night dive or for a novice open-water dive. Don't let this make you think that this dive is not worth doing, though, as that is certainly not the case. This little site has a lot to offer and macro-photographers will really enjoy it. I regularly dive this site making my way out to Johnstone's Hole (dive site 35) so you can enjoy two dives for the price of one. To find this site, walk around the harbour to the entry point, which is down a couple of steps to the left of the large cylindrical structure. To the right of this is the pebble beach which serves as the exit point. Entering the water from a flat platform on the left of the large cylindrical structure, you will find yourself in about 4 metres of water, depending on the tide. Take care to stick close to the reef wall and not to stray into the harbour entrance channel. Following the wall offshore, the depth increases and walls of orange-and-white dead man's fingers will appear. Soon, in a depth of around 7 metres, you will come across a blowhole forming a vertical shaft 1.5 metres in diameter, leading up to just below the surface. Here, butterfish can be seen feeding on mussels, and cowries are also in evidence. At high tide in calm conditions, the diver can fin up and through the blowhole. After this, a wall forms and shrimp and two-spot gobies are common sights in the cracks and crevices. Keep a look out for fifteen-spined sticklebacks as well. At the tip of the headland, at a depth of about 10 metres, large underwater boulders form a slope where conger eels can be found. At this point you have a choice: either fin round the headland and finish the dive on the pebble beach opposite the entry point, or continue the dive to encompass Johnstone's Hole. To get there, fin straight on when you get to the large rounded boulders, this will take you onto the inshore wall of Johnstone's Hole.

Dive no. 35

Name
Johnstone's Hole

Location
Dunbar harbour

Depth
6–14 metres

Conditions
Easy shore dive with good access. Care required crossing slippery boulders at low tide. Aim to dive this site at high water. On big spring tides, tidal movement can be strong on seaward side of dive site. Average visibility 6 metres

Access
Shore dive

Diver experience
Ocean diver

Butterfish at Johnstone's Hole

Dive site

Johnstone's Hole is an excellent shore-diving site, easily located and not too strenuous if you judge the tides well. After the walk around the harbour, past the entrance channel, you will come to a curved walkway. Here, on your right-hand side, you will see the Gripes, a large islet less than 100 metres offshore and known in diving circles as Johnstone's Hole. It is best to dive this site around high tide, cutting out the need to tread over 10 metres of large slippery boulders that make up a beach here. If you get it right, there are a few big rocks to sit on while you fit your fins, and then it's a short snorkel out to the rock. As you approach the rock, the bottom drops off to around 6 metres. In average conditions you will be able to see it and in summer the visibility can hit 15 metres here, but in the early season, unless there is a period of calm weather, the visibility does tend to fluctuate around the 4-metre mark. The dive begins and the wall drops straight down onto a seafloor of clean sand. A canopy of kelp grows above and behind you on the shallower reef. It's best to fin seawards from here in a clockwise fashion, keeping the wall on your right-hand side. You will soon note lots of recesses and contours in the wall and, after finning a short distance, the depth will start to increase. Here the walls start to become colonised and patches of orange-and-white dead man's fingers can be seen. The coverage increases as you fin around the northeastern tip of the island and if there is any sea running, you will now start to feel it, although only really big spring tides provide difficult finning conditions for the fit diver. At this point in the dive there is a feature on the seafloor like a gateway, inviting you through to the dive proper, and once this is passed, depth increases to around a maximum of 13 metres. Now, on the seaward side of the rock, cracks run up the wall opening into little caves and recesses. Just after the gateway, there are two such openings just where the wall hits the sand. In the first there is usually a lobster on guard duty, flexing its claws. On the other side of a small spur of rock, there is a slightly bigger opening which has had some surprising residents, notably a large cod. The wall is now really densely covered with dead man's fingers, and small butterfish scurry about trying to avoid the many scorpion fish. Here the wall curves round and it initially looks as if a gully is forming, but as you move forward you will note that you have entered a cave. This is home to large numbers of squat lobsters and edible crabs and, if you look above you, you will note codling lying at strange angles in a crack in the cave roof. Right at the back of the cave, which is only around 4 metres long, is a hole which usually has a lobster or two in residence, but take care not to stir up the silty seafloor. This little cave gives the dive its name but there is a more exciting part of the dive to come. Immediately as you exit the cave, there is a spur of rock to fin around before the sea floor drops a metre or so, forming a large steep-sided gully with walls rising a full 14 metres right up to the surface. It's really impressive finning through the 3-metre wide gap as the walls here are covered in life. It's here that you will spy nudibranchs and hermit crabs, as well as the ever-present scorpion fish. Passing through the gap, the seafloor rises and the gully opens out to form an amphitheatre and it's worth taking a bit of time to explore this area. I was certainly surprised to see a beautiful blue-and-gold male cuckoo wrasse here one day, as well as the more common ballan wrasse.

There is also a rather special physical feature here. Directly in front of you as you swim into the gully, a small crack runs up the wall. It's nothing special until it reaches 3 metres but then it opens out to a sizeable cave. I always get a slight sense of apprehension as I look in, as I have been surprised by a huge cod and more recently by a big conger eel. I certainly did not expect to see such large fish in such shallow water, but I wasn't complaining. In the early season, this is probably as far as you will wish to go as you may be getting cold. To get back to the exit point, just retrace your fin strokes, now keeping the wall on your left-hand side. As the summer wears on, you may wish to explore a little further around the island. Another gully can be seen, filled with large boulders. It has a ledge on the wall which is home to lobsters and edible crabs and it's not unusual to see a topknot here. You can circumnavigate the rock only at high tide so, after exploring the boulders, it's a good idea to return to the pebble beach by retracing your route. If you do attempt a night dive here and are unfamiliar with the underwater terrain, it is a good idea to have a shore party to guide you back to the pebble beach or to deploy a strobe to guide you back in, as its entry is narrow and obscured by cliffs on both sides.

This is an excellent site and is not over-dived. Local dive clubs use it as a training site on summer evenings and it can be popular at weekends, but it's nowhere near as busy as the sites at St Abbs further down the coast.

Dive no. 36

Scart Rock octopus

Name
Scart Rock

Location
Due north of Dunbar harbour entrance
GPS coordinates N5600.51 W0231.15

Depth
15 metres

Conditions
Average visibility 5 metres

Access
Boat only

Diver experience
Sports diver

Dive site
Scart Rock is a surprisingly good little dive site and is perfect for a second or third dive of the day. It lies due north of the end of the harbour fairway, 300 metres out to sea. Fishing trawlers tend to use the 100-metre wide channel between Scart Rock and Castlefoot Rock, which is the next rock to the east, as their passage through the chain of islands that lie off the harbour entrance, so it is therefore imperative to show the A

flag to warn passing boat traffic that divers are in the water. Equally, small boats should not block this channel. The dive itself is well worth the effort and is easy to navigate around. It's a small site in an average depth of 14 metres. Entering the water on the shoreward side of the rock and finning around in a clockwise direction, keep the wall on your right hand side. The walls drop off in a terraced effect. It is scenic diving and orange-and-white dead man's fingers cover the walls. Butterfish abound and this is one of the few sites where I have found a pogge, a small fish which resembles a scorpion fish but with rows of small barbels, sensors that help the fish locate food, hanging from the underside of its head. It also has two little hooks on the tip of its snout. Octopus are also common at this site and I found four on one short dive. I do not know why they like this area but I had never before seen so many on one site. Scart Rock must be prime real estate for them, possibly because this site is very rarely dived.

Dive no. 37

Name
Castlefoot Rock

Location
100 metres north of the north-west tip of Johnstone's Hole (dive site 35)
GPS coordinates N5600.49 W0231.03

Depth
14 metres

Yarrel's blenny at Castlefoot Rock

Conditions
Easy boat dive. Average visibility 5 metres

Access
Boat only

Diver experience
Sports diver

Dive site
Castlefoot Rock is a very similar dive to Scart Rock, although I would say less spectacular and slightly shallower. Marine life is also lacking in comparison with Scart Rock. Castlefoot Rock does, however, have some nice rock formations and cliff faces and I did note butterfish, Yarrel's blennies and lobster at this site, although no octopus. If you only have time for one dive, I would therefore suggest that Scart Rock is the better option, but if you want to tick off another site, Castlefoot Rock is worth the effort. It can easily be completed on a single tank of air in tandem with Scart Rock,

if you have time to fall twice off the RIB. This site does make an ideal site for divers undergoing training for their first dives out of a RIB, although you must always be mindful of the site's proximity to the harbour fairway. Although Castlefoot Rock is around 300 metres away from the harbour entrance, fishing trawlers and other small vessels use the 100-metre wide channel between Scart Rock and Castlefoot Rock as their access to the open sea, navigating through the small chain of islands that lies off Dunbar harbour. The Yetts (dive site 38) make a safer site in this respect, quite apart from being a vastly superior dive site, but Castlefoot Rock is completely under-dived and may hold a surprise for the inquisitive diver.

Dive no. 38

Plumose anemone and diver at the Yetts

Name
The Yetts

Location
200 metres offshore from Dunbar harbour
GPS coordinates N5600.54 W0230.65

Depth
11–18 metres

Conditions
Fantastic gullies. Average visibility 5 metres

Access
Best undertaken as a boat dive. Can be shore dived from Battery Reef but it is a very energetic snorkel out to the Yetts in tidal water

Diver experience
Sports diver

Dive site
Tantalisingly close to shore lie four attractive islands known as the Yetts. Being 200 metres offshore from the harbour, they are just within range for a snorkel by the fit diver, but the tidal flow can make this extremely hard work. These dives are therefore best undertaken as a boat dive, making diving the site a much easier affair and maximising your time on site. The Yetts are a quality dive site and deserve the effort needed to explore them. Running from west to east, the islands are basically in a line. There are

a few smaller islets here too, which show at different states of the tide. Starting at the westernmost end of the Yetts, there is a cracking dive around the two main islands here. Dropping down into a general depth of 12 metres, the walls fall straight to the seafloor. These walls are full of life and covered in bright soft corals. It will not be long before a split in the wall appears and a gully will open up. One fantastic and very narrow gully here stretches for between 20 and 30 metres, and for a part of its length the soft corals are replaced by beds of mussels. Average visibility at this site is around 5 metres, but the mussels filter the water and the visibility in this section of the gully noticeably clears. This is also the only dive site in the UK at which I have encountered squid. Finning on to the end of this gully, it appears to be a dead end. This, though, is not the case, as the wall turns at right angles and you emerge on the other side of the island. From here there are many more gullies to explore and it's easy to lose your bearings. This is a shallow site, though, so have fun if you have boat cover, although if you are shore-diving it is a bit more of a concern. The easternmost pair of islands make a similarly exciting dive with more fantastic gullies to be explored. If you are shore diving here, the eastern end of the easternmost island is where you are likely to end up and good gullies are to be found on the seaward side of this rock. High tide is the best time to shore-dive this site as it will enable you to get into deep water from the entry point at Battery Reef and minimise the length of the walk over kelp-covered boulders. Dunbar harbour dries around an hour each side of low tide, making launching a RIB difficult, so high tide makes this task easier as well. The Yetts are a superb site but they are completely under-dived, due to the need for a boat to dive them.

Battery Reef starfish

Dive no. 39

Name
Battery Reef

Location
Reef to northeast of Battery Fort (not Dunbar castle) at east end of harbour

Depth
10–12 metres depending on the tide

Conditions
Training site. Average visibility 5 metres

Access
Shore dive

Diver experience
Ocean diver

Dive site
Battery Reef is located behind the 18th-century Battery Fort at the east end of Dunbar harbour. The fort was built in 1781 to protect Dunbar from privateers after American ships tried to raid the harbour. This site is best accessed at high tide, minimising the amount of reef you have to clamber over before you get into the water. As a dive site it is fairly uninspiring and it is generally used as a training site or by divers looking for a lobster for the pot. Divers sometimes alternate their return from Johnstone's Hole (dive site 35) to take in this reef, although this has never been an attractive option to me. My only interest in the site has been when making my way to and from the Yetts (dive site 38) which lie offshore from this site. There are just so many superior shore dives in the area that I would say that Battery Reef should be regarded purely as a training site. General depths are 10 metres and the sea floor is flat and sandy, dotted with large boulders covered in kelp. Edible crabs and lobsters can be found beneath these and will make exciting finds for the brand new diver.

The beautiful reef at Siccar Rock

Dive no. 40

Name
Siccar Rock

Location
One mile offshore from Siccar Point
GPS coordinates N5600.82 W0228.61

Depth
8–32 metres

Conditions
Fantastic underwater pinnacle. Average visibility 8 metres

Access
Boat only

Diver experience
Sports diver/dive leader

Dive site
The pinnacle known as Siccar Rock is roughly the size of a

football pitch, at its shallowest point reaching to within 8 metres of the surface. It is generally bare rock covered in hydroids and it is here that you can find many types of nudibranch, while families of ballan wrasse can be seen in these shallow areas too. A plateau is reached at 16 metres and this section abounds with schooling fish. I have been dropped onto the pinnacle thinking that I am descending into a kelp bed, the fronds waving in the tide, but found that in fact I was descending into a massive school of pollack and coalfish obscuring the top of the pinnacle, their tails moving like swaying kelp. At the edge of the plateau the wall drops away to the seafloor at 32 metres. It is covered with orange-and-white dead man's fingers and plumose anemones and is quite a spectacular sight. Octopus are often found hiding between the boulders at the base of the cliff, which does not drop vertically at all points of the compass. Sometimes there is a terraced affect where the wall falls in a series of juts, as at the east side of the pinnacle. Moving around with the wall at your right shoulder, the wall becomes vertical as you reach the south and southwestern faces and here the most spectacular diving is to be found. I am led to believe that the walls along the northern side of the pinnacle are gentler in nature. Another interesting point about this site is that ancient stone anchors have been found and lifted from here. Some of these have been passed to the Dunbar Town Museum to be displayed, so, if diving this site, keep an eye out for more of these relics. They are said to be triangular in form with a round hole in the top and were used to moor small fishing boats over the site in ancient times. Angling is still popular here today and be aware of some discarded tackle at the site, although it's generally not a problem for divers. Siccar Rock may be a place that is to be avoided by the big vessels plying up and down the Firth of Forth but for vast amounts of marine life it is home, and divers should not miss the chance to dive this excellent scenic site.

Dive no. 41

Name
Cyclops

Location
5 km northeast of Dunbar
GPS coordinates N5603.45
W0232.17

Depth
42–44 metres

Conditions
Average visibility 8 metres. Can
reach 15 metres in good conditions

Access
Boat only

Diver experience
Experienced sports diver/dive
leader

Dive site
The *Cyclops* sank in heavy seas in
1924 on her way to be scrapped,
which is excellent news for
divers. She was a 180-foot long
barge-dredger. The *Cyclops* had
no means of self-propulsion and
needed to be towed by another
vessel. She now lies in 40–42
metres of water and makes an
excellent dive. She lies heavily
listed over on her side, virtually

Dredging bucket with dahlia anemone

upside down, but the bucket and gantry system can still clearly be seen. This is an
interesting system which you can follow around on a dive. There are the huge cogs
that drove the system, all powered by a large boiler which today is home to lobsters
and Yarrel's blennies, which live in the pipe work. The dredging buckets make perfect
homes for bigger lobsters, so keep your eyes peeled for large specimens inhabiting every one of the scoops. Bib are always found in large numbers around the wreck, forming
small schools. I always like seeing them as the dark bands on their flanks make them
an attractive fish. Their numbers suggest that the *Cyclops* must suit them very well, and

they grow to a large size. I really enjoy this dive as she is an unusual wreck and I find her dredging gear interesting to explore. This wreck also lies on a sandy seafloor and in good conditions and with the plentiful marine life that inhabits the wreck, it can be a very scenic dive. Apart from the depth and tide, the only other hazards are a trawl net wrapped around one end of the barge and, in late summer, the huge lion's mane jellyfish that drift in the strong tides, making deco stops very interesting indeed.

Dive no. 42

U-74e conning tower; note also porthole and wiper blade

Name
U-74e

Location
5 km out of Dunbar
GPS coordinates N5603.70
W0229.71

Depth
42–47 metres

Conditions
Visibility 6–15 metres

Access
Boat only

Diver experience
Dive leader/advanced diver

Dive site
Until the recent finds of more German U-boats in the Firth of Forth, *U-74E* was the ultimate submarine dive in the area and, while the new finds and K-boats do now steal the show, it still makes for a cracking dive. *U-74E*, which was found in 1993, was a German Imperial World War One mine-laying submarine. She lies in 40–47 metres of water, depending on the state of the tide. Her bows are raised to an angle of about 30 degrees. Her stern is either buried in the mud or, more likely, has been dispersed. Because of this, no conclusive identification of the vessel has ever been made. The wreck sinks into the silt just aft of her deck gun, where the rotten

planking of her raised walkway can be seen. This provides a home for a large conger eel. You can view the eel's entire length through the gaps in the planking. This area is just aft of the wrecks conning tower, which rises up about 5 metres and has two periscopes. Covered in orange-and-white plumose anemones, this makes a dramatic scene back-lit by the green water. Small brass portholes can be seen on the conning tower, each with their little brass wiper blade. In front of the conning tower are the remains of a winch which was used to raise the submarines, two masts and an aerial to enable radio communication. The submarine's outer plating has mainly rotted away, exposing the pressure hull. Schools of bib flirt between the hull and the raised deck planking of the walkway, trod by German submariners all those years ago.

Moving further towards the bow, divers will pass an escape hatch which is still locked up tight. A few metres in front of the hatch is the rear hatch of the torpedo tube, situated in the port side of the casing at the bow of the wreck. Dropping over the hull here, the diver can fin around the bow. Take care, though, as there is a trawl net here on the port side of the wreck. It's also here that the torpedo can be seen. If you have time, check for ling hiding in the space between the underside of the bow and the seafloor. Moving around to the starboard side of the wreck and finning aft, the diver will fin into the forward hydroplane which is situated a few metres back from the bow. The oval hydroplane is in the diving position, surrounded by a rectangular guard. These are great structures to have a look at. Rising back up to deck level and heading back to the conning tower and the safety of the shotline, the tour of the visible remains of *U-74E* is complete. I often wonder what has happened to the vessel's stern section which will be around the same size again as the bow section. Does it lie beneath the mud, never to be seen again? There are rumours that the stern is lying not far away to the south of the wreck's bow section. Although I would like this to be the case, I find it unlikely, as the site has been well searched by divers hoping to find the dredger *Cyclops* (dive site 41) or the bow section of *U-74E*. It is, though, a big sea out there so you never know.

The boiler of the River Garry *wreck*

Dive no. 43

Name
River Garry

Location
One mile offshore from Torness
power station, east of Dunbar
GPS coordinates N5559.84
W0225.07

Depth
25–28 metres

Conditions
Broken shipwreck. Average
visibility 8 metres

Access
Boat only

Diver experience
Sports diver/dive leader

Dive site
I first dived the *River Garry* in
1990, just a month or so after
it was rediscovered by divers.
At that time, portholes were
still visible, trapped beneath
steel plates. The same applied
to the bell, which was retrieved
in a slightly crushed state a few
months later. The wreck had
been salvaged in the 1940s by
the great grandfather of Iain

Easingwood of Marine Quest, who was a salvage diver on this wreck. The *River Garry*
sank in hurricane-force winds in November 1893. All hands were lost and it must
have been terrifying as the ship succumbed to the storm and sank into the cold winter waters of the Firth of Forth. Since the wreck was rediscovered, she has been well
plundered. I even remember seeing a large yellow railways van being loaded up with
tonnes of brass piping from the wreck. Needless to say, the wreck today is completely
flattened. Her engine and one of her boilers are still intact and, for me, these large
structures are the most impressive remains. The plates lie flat across the seabed on
either side of the keel and massive cradles on which the boilers were once mounted

can be seen. The wreckage generally has sparse coverings of marine life, apart from the single large boiler which opposes the tide and is covered in soft corals. Large fish are found on this wreck and very large pollack cruise around the remains. Make a point of checking beneath the plates as I have seen massive ling hiding here. Ballan wrasse flirt around the boiler and the engine block. I have also noted what appears to be a white hard coral growing on this wreck. Moving forward towards the bow, the wreckage thins out a bit but there are mooring bollards and some nice anchors that make great photographic props. The bow itself is completely flattened and hawse pipes lie on the sea floor near a large cargo winch. The *River Garry* may not be the Forth's most colourful wreck but there is still a lot of marine life inhabiting her remains and she makes a very worthwhile dive.

Dive no. 44

School of fish on the wreck of Scotia

Name
Scotia

Location
Offshore from Peas Bay
GPS coordinates unavailable. Contact Marine Quest to arrange dive

Depth
47 metres

Conditions

Deep dark dive. Average visiblity 8 metres

Access

Boat only

Diver experience

Advanced diver

Dive site

In December 2006, whilst investigating a mystery shipwreck, dive operators Marine Quest dropped me, along with two rebreather divers, onto an unidentified shipwreck. My mission was to identify the wreck. It soon became clear to me that it was a dredging vessel of some type, which made identification somewhat easier. Wreck researcher Martin Sinclair discovered that it was the *Scotia*, which foundered in huge seas in 1893 while being towed from Eyemouth to Granton. The wreck lies on a coarse sand and mud seafloor from which the wreck rises 4 metres. Visibility at the site is generally good at around the 8-metre mark but the water is dark. For some reason not much ambient light filters down to this wreck, even on sunny days. Diving here is superb and as the diver nears the wreck, large schools of juvenile whiting can be seen darting through the wreckage. It is extremely difficult to orientate yourself at first, as the forward section of the wreck is a latticework of spars where the steel plates have fallen away to the seafloor. Marine life plasters these spars of steel and beautiful orange-and-white dead man's fingers and plumose anemones fight for space. That school of juvenile whiting appears to follow the diver around the wreck as they swarm around in vast numbers. Perhaps you, like me, will hear from rebreather divers that fish disappear when a noisy bubble-making open circuit diver turns up on the scene. I was definitely blowing bubbles but the fish were going nowhere, as far as I could see. It is superb.

Marine Quest operates a non-retrieval-of-artefacts policy when diving with them, unless it is a feature like the bell that can be used to positively identify the wreck. At the very prow of the ship I found a large rectangular glass lens, probably from a light fitting. Then, between the spars, I noted a brass porthole lying in the mud along with a broken china plate. This last item bore no clues to help with the identification of the wreck. All these artefacts were left in place and you should be able to see them too when you dive this wreck. Moving aft along the port side, the hull re-forms somewhat and the collapsed bucket gantry comes into view. As on the wreck of the *Cyclops* (dive site 41), the buckets are prime real estate as every one is home to a large lobster, which flex their claws at divers as they pass by. Rising up to the re-formed deck, a massive cog that powered the bucket gantry is visible as are slightly smaller horizontal ones. The mast has fallen down and now lies over the starboard hull. Right at the stern of the wreck is an anchor. As the *Scotia* had no means of self-propulsion, there is neither rudder nor propeller on this wreck. Turning around to retrace your route back to the bow and the shotline, you have a great chance to fin forward through the narrow hopper. This once contained all the dredged material but now is just another space to be filled by those juvenile whiting. It's fantastic to fin through the school of fish. I even noted a few Yarrel's blennies and butterfish nestling in the soft corals. The *Scotia* is a superb dive, if a little dark, and the chance of seeing artefacts in place always gives the diver an extra buzz.

Dive no. 45

Sabbia *wreck divers decompressing*

Name
Sabbia

Location
8 miles east-northeast of Dunbar
GPS coordinates N5604.56 W0218.09

Depth
55 metres

Conditions
Deep wreck dive, visibility 5–15 metres

Access
Boat only. Contact Marine Quest

Diver experience
Technical diver

Dive site

The steamship *Sabbia* was built on the Clyde in 1908 but was, however, in the employment of an enemy nation and impounded at the start of World War One. When hostilities started, she was refused permission to leave Newcastle upon Tyne where she was berthed. At just over 100 metres long and 2800 gross tons, the *Sabbia* was soon requisitioned by the Admiralty and put to work as a collier. On 20 April 1916 she was steaming through the cold waters of the Firth of Forth when she hit a mine and slowly started to settle before quietly slipping beneath the waves. The mine, interestingly enough, was laid by the German submarine *U-74E* (dive site 42). *U-74E* was herself sunk on her next mission, less than a month after her mines sunk the *Sabbia*, and now lies on the seafloor a few miles from her victim. The shallowest section of the *Sabbia* is said to be around 46 metres and this was the section on which I was aiming to dive. The shotline, however, landed on a flattened section of the wreck standing only one metre proud of the 55-metre deep seabed. This restricted my exploration somewhat, but I soon found where the hull reformed and immediately noted a massive winch beside a large hold, full of coal. On finning along the deck back to the shotline, I noted that the wreck ended in a straight line, suggesting that a section of the wreck had been blown off in an explosion. To my eyes it looked as if the wreck had been cut open as the break was so straight. I wondered if any salvage work had been carried out on the *Sabbia*, although this seems unlikely as her cargo was coal. This is a big dive and the stern is said to be intact, forming the shallowest point of the wreck. If you can guarantee that the shotline will find this section of the wreck, then diving on air is possible. I would suggest, though, that diving the wreck on trimix will make for a much more memorable and enjoyable experience.

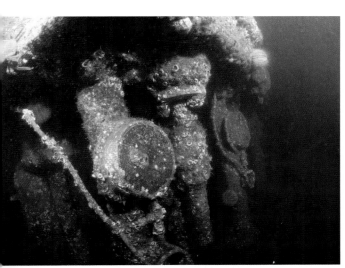

Gauges on the Dove *wreck*

Dive no. 46

Name
Dove

Location
1 mile northwest of Fast Castle, St Abbs
GPS coordinates unavailable.
Contact Marine Quest to arrange dive.

Depth
43 metres

Conditions
Shipwreck on silty seafloor

Visibility often 10 metres but deteriorates with divers on wreck

Access

Boat only. Contact Marine Quest

Diver experience

Advanced diver/technical diver

Dive site

This shipwreck was found at the beginning of 2008, but no conclusive evidence has surfaced to confirm its identity. Iain Easingwood of Marine Quest firmly believes that it is the whaling vessel *Dove*. I tend to agree with him but have talked to some divers on surfacing who dispute that the wreck is a whaler. This debate is likely to rumble on until some form of evidence is uncovered to confirm the wreck's identity. The *Dove* was sunk in 1883 when she was caught by a hurricane in the North Sea. In the raging tempest, visibility was reduced to nothing and any vessels caught in the storm found it impossible to navigate. When the storm abated, the *Dove* had disappeared and nobody was witness to where she had sunk beneath the waves. Has the final resting place of this vessel at last been found?

The *Dove* is a very nice wreck to dive although the silty seafloor does tend to silt the wreck up. On this wreck, early preparation does pay, so be ready to get onto the wreck quickly. The visibility on this wreck is variable within a 5–15 metres range. Dropping down the line on a good day, the diver will be able to make out a ship-shaped wreck on the seafloor, with the engine block and boiler being the most substantial remains. The shotline will have landed near these features. Try to slow your descent so that you don't hit the seafloor, or the fine silt will plume up around you, significantly decreasing the visibility. Landing in front of the boiler, there is a lot for the diver to explore, even stairs leading down into the hull of the ship which is buried under the mud. Schools of bib and small pollack school around this most prominent section of the wreck. Finning aft, the engine block comes into view and the diver will note some fine brass portholes, with glass intact, lying on the seafloor. Marine Quest's policy that items should not be removed will, I hope, ensure that these portholes remain to thrill divers of the future, rather than be taken to lie in somebody's garage. Finning around onto the starboard side of the engine, two of the engineer's gauges are still in place. It will be the first chance for many divers to see this type of artefact still visible on a shipwreck. Aft of the engine block, the deck has disintegrated and lies below the mud. Only a small piece of the gunnels rises above the seafloor, marking the outline of the wreck. Mooring bollards can be seen and two cradles, which may have carried the ship's small boats, are also present. A spare propeller along with an anchor and large winch are visible near the stern. Finning forward, passing the engine and boiler, there is once again no sign of the deck although a hatch combing is visible. There are more mooring bollards and another winch, and vast quantities of coal cover the seafloor. This is an interesting dive and this small wreck still offers a lot for the diver to see. I hope we will soon know for sure whether or not this wreck is, in fact, the *Dove*.

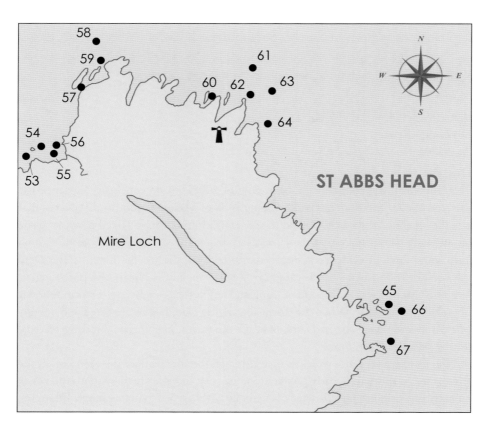

ST ABBS HEAD

Mire Loch

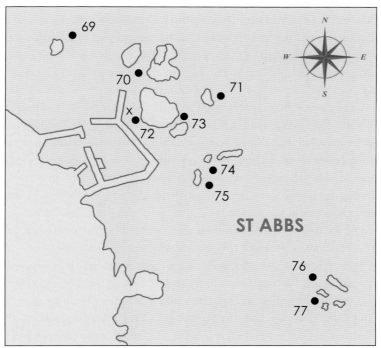

ST ABBS

x–Entry/exit point for shore dives

ST ABBS

St Abbs, which lies 45 miles southeast of Edinburgh, is a charming place and a fantastic dive destination, held in high regard around the world. It is probably the best shore-diving destination in Scotland, if not the whole of the UK, and certainly offers my favourite shore dive, around and about Cathedral Rock. There are currently four dive boats operating out of St Abbs which will visit the sites in the immediate area, from Ebb Carrs to the sites around St Abbs Head and Pettico Wick. The sites further afield are visited by Marine Quest based in Eyemouth and only some of the St Abbs boats. Check when you book if you wish to visit these sites. The diving is generally scenic diving of superb quality but there are a couple of scenic shipwrecks of note. St Abbs itself is a quaint village nestled around a picturesque harbour. Most of the dive boat operators offer accommodation either at St Abbs or in the nearby village of Coldingham, around a mile away. St Abbs itself has a couple of cafés that are open only during the day but Coldingham has a few pubs where you can get bar meals. It's also in Coldingham that you will find Scoutscroft Holiday Park and Dive Centre. Air is available both here and at St Abbs harbour itself. St Abbs Head also forms part of the St Abbs and Eyemouth Voluntary Marine Reserve. Protected waters stretch south from Pettico Wick to Eyemouth.

Parking charges apply at the harbour. Rates are per hour but whole day parking currently costs £7

St Abbs harbour

Dive no. 47

Exploring HMS Pathfinder

Name
HMS *Pathfinder*

Location
10 miles off St Abbs Head
GPS coordinates unavailable. Contact Marine Quest to arrange dive

Depth
61 metres to the deck, seabed 67 metres

Conditions
Superb historic wreck covered in artefacts. Average visibility a dark 6 metres

Access
Boat only. Contact Marine Quest

Diver experience
Technical diver

Dive site
HMS *Pathfinder* was a 2940-ton, Scout-class light cruiser and is another of the extremely important historic shipwrecks in the Firth of Forth. She was the first warship ever to be sunk by a torpedo fired from a submarine.

The morning of 5 September 1914 dawned clear and the conditions made the belching black smoke from HMS *Pathfinder's* three funnels visible for miles around. She was patrolling the outer Firth of Forth with a flotilla of destroyers and torpedo boats. The patrol was to last for five days, which caused problems for HMS *Pathfinder*. Coal shortages at the outbreak of World War One and the poor endurance of this class of ship meant that HMS *Pathfinder* needed to cruise at five knots to complete her patrol, or else run out of fuel. The sea was mirror calm and the afternoon sunlight shone down. The gentle progress of the light cruiser had been monitored for some time by Kapitänleutnant Otto Hersing, who was in command of the German submarine *U-21*. He had soon tracked the vessel by the black smoke from her stacks. HMS *Pathfinder* was a sitting duck and Hersing fired a torpedo from around 4000 yards off HMS *Pathfinder's* starboard bow. The torpedo was seen and tracked by the lookouts as it raced towards the ship but they were powerless to evade it. At five knots, HMS *Pathfinder* was making so little headway that when orders to avoid the torpedo were given, the ship would not respond to the helm, unable to steer effectively at such slow speeds. The torpedo struck just below the forward guns and ignited the cordite in the magazines. The bow vaporised and HMS *Pathfinder* started to settle very quickly. Fearing that the explosion had not been observed by the remaining ships of the flotilla, the captain ordered that a blank shell be fired from the stern gun. All but nine of her 268 crew lost their lives.

Diving the wreck, which lies at 60–67 metres, requires technical diving skills. HMS *Pathfinder* is the main reason I undertook such training, as this ship's history drew me like a magnet to explore its remains. Visibility is usually 5–10 metres, but dark. Descending the shotline, it's a long way down and all ambient light is left behind as the depth increases. Divers usually stop to attach a strobe to the shotline to assist in relocating it after the dive. At a depth of 61 metres, the diver lands on the deck just aft of the remains of the bridge. Voice pipes and levers can be seen here. Finning aft along the port side of the wreck takes the diver past torpedo tubes, and shells lie on the deck. Some are packed in groups of six, their wooden box having rotted around them. Portholes also lie on the deck. There are more mundane items to be seen as well, such as mooring bollards and capstans. Nearing the stern, a large 4-inch gun points towards the surface in an elevated position. This could be the gun that fired the blank shell to try to alert nearby ships to the plight of HMS *Pathfinder*. At the stern, a large anchor lies on the deck, and if the diver drops over the stern they will be able to view the twin screws in a depth of 67 metres. Returning to the shotline, back up the starboard side of the wreck, more ordnance is noted as well as guns pulled from their mounts. This is most likely the work of trawl nets and there are the remains of some nets on the wreck.

Just aft of the bridge is one of the most poignant sights I have ever seen underwater. On the deck a brass sextant glowed green in my torchlight. Guns and portholes are all magnificent sights but this sextant would have been used by one of the ship's crew, who most likely lost his life on that day. It really brought home the human aspect of the dive. HMS *Pathfinder* is obviously a war grave and should be treated with the utmost respect.

Very recently, Iain and Jim Easingwood of Marine Quest have located and put divers onto the remains of the bow section of HMS *Pathfinder*. This was thought to have been completely destroyed in the explosion. Reports from Iain suggest that there is a section of the wreckage rising out of the seafloor to a height of one metre. I have not yet visited this site and it has been added to my ever-expanding wish list of dives to be completed in the Firth of Forth. For the technical diver, HMS *Pathfinder* makes an outstanding dive.

Dive no. 48

Wolffish at Fast Castle

Name
Fast Castle

Location
North of St Abbs Head
GPS coordinates N5556.02
W0213.43

Depth
12–22 metres

Conditions
Superb gullies. Average
visibility 10 metres

Access
Boat only. Contact Marine Quest

Diver experience
Ocean diver

Dive site
Not much remains of Fast Castle today, but what is left will allow an imaginative person to picture how it may once have looked. The history of this small castle is impressive. While King James V was still too young to take the throne, Cardinal Beaton became Regent and ruled Scotland. In his time he did much to save Scotland from the English king, Henry VIII: these were the dangerous times of Rough Wooing, with Henry attempting to win Scotland through a combination of military might and then later in the minority of Mary Queen of Scots matchmaking. Soon Cardinal Beaton was in hiding in a cave directly beneath Fast Castle. Rumour had it that he held a vast fortune in gold there.

I had a snorkel into the cave and a look around inside, but the slippery rocks were too dangerous for a diver on his own.

With this wonderful mixture of history and scenery colouring the scene, divers can't wait to get into the water. The first site, right under the castle, doesn't warrant a mention. It's just a kelpy boulder-filled scour, with a complete lack of life and – honestly – no gold.

Move offshore 200 metres and it's a different story. Here, beautiful sand-filled gullies, full of life, run down from 12 to 17 metres. I found five wolffish on a single dive here recently and this is now one of the best places to see these fish. As you pass 18 metres, the seafloor flattens out somewhat and becomes overrun by brittle stars interspersed with fantastically-coloured dahlia anemones. This continues down to a depth of around 22 metres, but it's likely that the diver will wish to return to the superb gullies and explore for wolffish amongst the dead man's fingers. Cod and ling are common here too, and the diver should always keep a lookout for smaller Yarrel's blennies that are common at this site. If you are diving with Marine Quest, Jim and Iain will know exactly where to drop you in the water. The rule of thumb here is to get into slightly deeper water of, say, 15 metres: optimum wolffish-spotting depth is 15–18 metres. After experiencing a few poor dives around the castle, I was delighted to dive the reef 200 metres offshore. It is a fantastic site and rivals the Brander (dive site 51) as the best dive in the area.

Ballan wrasse and sea urchin on Nyon *wreck*

Dive no. 49

Name
Nyon

Location
Between The Souter and Fast Castle
GPS coordinates N5555.93 W0212.98

Depth
Wreckage at 6–15 metres

Conditions
Nice shallow site. Average visibility 10 metres

Access
Boat only

Diver experience
Ocean diver

Dive site
On 17 November 1958, the Swiss motor vessel *Nyon* didn't get very far on her voyage

from Leith to Dakar. After only 40 miles, 5000 tonnes of potential shipwreck was sitting high and dry on Meg Watson's Rocks, just north of The Souter. Over the next 11 days, salvage experts tried to save the ship, but bad weather hindered the tugs' attempts to drag the *Nyon* free. Rather than have the ship become a total loss, it was decided to cut her in half amidships. This was completed successfully and the intact stern section was towed to Tynemouth shipyard, where it was fitted to a new bow section. This ship would sink three years later in the English Channel. The original bow remained on Meg Watson's Rocks until the first storm of December swept the bridge from the wreck and broke the ship up. The bow section was sold to salvagers who took it piece by piece up the cliff, but what was left behind now lies at 6–15 metres. It's a very scenic spot, with red fronds of kelp wafting above the gullies. Ballan wrasse fin about, using the huge steel girders that litter the sea floor as cover. I soon found winches and a fire hose reel, and then one of the *Nyon*'s massive anchors. Examining a photo of the stranded ship, it was easy, by looking down the anchor chain, to pinpoint exactly where I had been diving. There was certainly plenty of wreckage to see and with information gained from the photo, there appears to be potential for even more wreckage further out. It would also be more visible in the deeper water, as it would not be shrouded in kelp. I really enjoyed this dive because of its scenic beauty, and diving the wreckage of a ship whose loss was extremely well-documented is always interesting. She makes a cracking second or third dive of the day and there is certainly potential for making new finds after the winter storms have shifted the sandy seafloor.

The Souter nudibranch

Dive no. 50

Name
The Souter

Location
4.5 km northwest of Pettico Wick. Highly visible sea stack.

Depth
10–20 metres

Conditions
Easy diving. Average visibility 8 metres

Access
Boat only

Diver experience
Ocean diver/sports diver

Dive site

The Souter is another prominent landmark of the area. It's a sea stack and looks like a miniature version of the Old Man of Hoy. A large shallow reef runs offshore from the stack, just breaking the surface at points, and it is at the end of this reef that depth increases rapidly to 20 metres. Here you will find large sandy-floored gullies that form homes for lobsters. It's a fairly scenic spot but not as dramatic as the Brander (dive site 51) or Fast Castle (dive site 48). Retracing my fin strokes back into around 10 metres of water, beautiful kelp-fringed gullies opened up, running in a northwesterly direction from the Souter stack itself. I found these gullies far prettier and richer in marine life than the deeper ones. The Souter can therefore offer two levels of diving. I personally would opt for the shallower gullies at this site, but you have the choice. In the shallows, two gullies opened up. I decided to explore first the one on the left, and soon I came across a length of anchor chain running the length of the 30-metre long gully, culminating in a large iron anchor and other remains of an ancient sailing ship. I happily finned around for half an hour, noting small bits of wreckage. There were lots of small nudibranchs here too, and schools of small pollack darted through the kelp on the top of the gullies. The Souter is a pretty site with plenty of marine life and wreckage to identify. The shallow gullies are excellent for photography.

Dive no. 51

Edible crab

Name
The Brander

Location
4 km northwest of Pettico Wick. Large finger of rock pointing straight out to sea for 250 metres

Depth
9–27 metres

Conditions
Great wall dive on north side, fantastic gullies on south side. Average visibility 10 metres

Access
Boat only

Diver experience
Sports diver

Dive site
The Brander is a massive finger of rock that sticks out at right angles to the sea cliffs. It points out to the northeast for around 250 metres before slipping under the water and continuing down to a maximum depth of 27 metres at the end the reef.

This is a big site and there is a lot to explore. There is much more to it than you can see on the surface. The walls to the north and south are completely different in terms of the marine life which inhabits them. Both sides make excellent but completely different dives.

Starting on the north side, enter the water around halfway along the visible bit of the Brander. Further inshore, gullies form and large groups of ballan wrasse flirt about in the kelp. They are inquisitive but in no way as tame as the wrasse found at the usual St Abbs sites. The best dive is to head out into deeper water with the intention of rounding the submerged point of the Brander. Dropping straight down the near-vertical north wall to 16 metres, a clean sandy seafloor abuts the smooth rock. This is a continuation of what you can see on land.

Underwater, the sun shines down through the bright green water and lion's mane jellyfish drift overhead. Without looking too hard you will note pollack and solitary ballan wrasse. The wall is completely encrusted in brittle stars punctuated by sea urchins and massive dinner-plate sized dahlia anemones. On a good day you can look straight up the wall and see the surface. As you fin out to sea, the seafloor drops away and you can either decide to make your maximum depth 18 metres, or follow the seafloor and end up at 27 metres. I prefer the first option as it maximises my time at the site, but it's completely up to you and there are interesting creatures to be found deeper on the wall. Fin on for another 50 metres and enjoy all the cracks and fissures that are home to edible crabs, squat lobsters and the odd leopard-spotted goby. It's here that the reef top slopes down to reach a depth of 18 metres and you can take advantage of a deep crack to break through to the south side of the Brander. At first, all you will see is a hole opening up in the top of the reef, just begging to be explored. The first swathes of plumose anemones are noted here, along with a few mating velvet-backed swimming crabs. Follow the crack through the reef and you will emerge at the south side, where the dull brittle stars give way to glorious coverings of dead man's fingers. It's such a contrast to the north side, like starting another dive with the lights turned on. The deep, moody, smooth walls of the north side give way to shrouds of orange-and-white dead man's fingers thriving in the sunlit water of the south-facing side. I personally have never noted such an extreme change of marine life on a single dive as I have at the Brander. It is a huge site and here you will find yourself in a gully rather than on the other side of the Brander. What appears to happen is that the long single finger of rock seen above the surface splits into fingers once submerged, creating a series of very impressive gullies. These have walls that rise up almost to the surface and every square centimetre is a gorgeous blaze of orange-and-white dead man's fingers. Finning back inshore, this gully narrows to about 4 metres in width. Pollack lazily glide in front of you and octopus do their best to hide, imitating the dead man's fingers. At points, the south wall of the gully drops down, enabling you to fin over to the next gully. There are a couple of really nice gullies here. Rising over the wall of the last one, you will see that the seafloor is full of large rounded boulders and that kelp starts to take over. At this point I like to fin back to one of the previous gullies and fin up the ridge found between two adjoining gullies. It's like being on some Alpine ridge walk, but better. Fin up the ridge to your deco stops and fire up your delayed surface marker buoy to let the boat know where you are. This is certainly one of the best dives to be found to the north of St Abbs Head. Marine Quest regularly bring their boat up here from Eyemouth and some of the St Abbs boats will come up here, but do check first to avoid disappointment.

Thrummy Carr

Dive no. 52

Name
Thrummy Carr, St Abbs

Location
The next point west from Pettico Wick
GPS coordinates N5554.96 W0209.74

Depth
10–17 metres

Conditions
Scenic dive. Average visibility 5 metres

Access
Boat only

Diver experience
Ocean diver/sports diver

Dive site

As with all the sites around the Pettico Wick area, Thrummy Carr can be a sheltered site when wind or swell arrives from an easterly direction. This is a site favoured by macro- and close-up photographers. The site consists of a tumble of large boulders and cliffs down to a depth of around 12 metres. Kelp covers the top of these features and, as depth increases, dead man's fingers take over. Schools of pollack dart along the reef and large numbers of two-spotted gobies school close to the rocks. Perfect food and territory, then, for the ambush predator fish, the John Dory. Moving away from the cliffs, fingers of rock 1.5 metres high run out over the coarse sand-and-shell seafloor, providing a home for lots of small marine creatures such as pink shrimp and spider crabs. I didn't find this the most exciting of dives, possibly because I had intended to dive the *Glanmire*, but an easterly swell ruled that site out. I was stuck with a wide-angle set-up in this macro-heaven. This is an ideal site for novices and macro-photographers and anybody who would like to see a John Dory.

Dive no. 53

A flounder at the Letterbox

Name
The Letterbox, St Abbs

Location
First point west of Pettico Wick

GPS coordinates N5554.90 W0209.27

Depth
10–17 metres

Conditions
Easy dive with interesting tunnel. Average visibility 5 metres

Access
Shore and boat. Very long fin from shore, boat dive advised.

Shore access via road to St Abbs lighthouse (veer left off road 400 metres prior to reaching st abbs harbour). Divers' car park on left of road. Path in poor state of repair down steep slope to slipway

Diver experience
Ocean diver/sports diver

Dive site
It is a long way to fin to dive this site from the shore. I inadvertently managed to do it once while taking a look around the reef past the boilers of the *Odense* (dive site 54). The Letterbox is only around 40 metres further on past them. As the Letterbox is partially obscured by a large boulder, it can be difficult to find the opening on the seaward side. Because of the long fin and the difficulty of finding the site, the easiest way by far of exploring this site is by boat. Dive boats will drop you metres from the shoreward entrance. The Letterbox is a horizontal tunnel around 8 metres long, 4 metres wide and perhaps 2 metres in depth. It is roughly rectangular in shape, hence the name, and the tunnel itself is in shallow water of 8–10 metres and full of life. This, though, makes up only a very small piece of the dive. Once you emerge from the seaward side of the tunnel you can fin in any direction you choose, if you have boat cover. I generally decide to descend to where the reef meets the sand in a depth of around 17 metres. I then turn east and follow the reef back around into Pettico Wick. Where the reef meets the sand, there are some magnificently-coloured dahlia anemones and burrowing anemones to be found here. Flatfish abound although they are hard to see at first. I like to run my fingers through the sand as I fin along, as it's amazing what jumps out in front of you: Northern prawns, common shrimp, flatfish, dragonets and gobies. All are almost invisible before being disturbed, when their movement gives them away. As the tide here is less of an issue, the coverings of soft corals are much patchier than the complete colonisation found at the sites around St Abbs Head. If you keep following the edge of the reef along this route, you will invariably run into the boilers of the *Odense* (dive site 54) where some larger pollack and ballan wrasse will be observed.

The Letterbox, like all the sites in Pettico Wick Bay, makes a good substitute dive site when fog or easterly wind or swell is affecting sites around St Abbs Head and the harbour area.

Diver investigates boiler

Dive no. 54

Name
Odense

Location
Pettico Wick bay
GPS coordinates N5554.90
W0209.19

Depth
13–16 metres maximum

Conditions
Easy wreck dive from the shore,
quite a long fin. Average
visibility 5 metres

Access
Shore access via road to St
Abbs lighthouse (veer left off
road 400 metres prior to
reaching St Abbs harbour).
Divers' car park on left of road.
Path in poor state of repair
down steep slope to slipway.

Diver experience
Ocean diver/sports diver

Dive site

Off St Abbs Head in 1917, the German submarine *UC-77* had the steamship *Odense* in the crosshairs of its periscope. A torpedo was fired but the *Odense* was lucky and the danger passed her by. *UC-77* then surfaced and attacked the ship with its deck gun, killing two of the crew. Luck on the *Odense* was running out as the power failed and the ship started to drift into Pettico Wick Bay. Thankfully, *UC-77* quickly departed on the arrival of a British aircraft. The *Odense* grounded and hopes that she could be saved came to nothing when a storm swept the coast and she broke up. The ship was carrying a cargo of monkey nuts, earning the wreck the nickname 'The Peanut Boat' in diving circles.

To dive this wreck, head out northwest to a rock which breaks the surface120 metres from your position on the jetty at Pettico Wick. This rock is called Wick Gaut. This is basically the same dive plan as for diving Pettico Wick (dive site 55). Descend when you have enough water under you. The seafloor will be covered in small boulders and it won't take you long to notice some broken rusty spars and plates that once were the *Odense*. Keep an eye out for angler fish too. Once you are in 10–12 metres of water and start to note sand covering the seafloor on your right (offshore) side, turn 90 degrees and fin offshore. Depth will increase and depending on the tide, you will run into a large boiler standing on its end in 14–16 metres of water. Kelp covers the top of the boiler which is also usually surrounded by a school of pollack. The bottom section of the boiler has gaping holes in it and investigation usually turns up ballan wrasse hiding inside. Two boilers are the only remaining features of the wreck that can easily be identified. The rest of the ship, apart from the odd bollard, has been completely smashed to pieces and now lies encrusted with seaweed and kelp.

This site is nice and shallow and you will have time to cross the sandy patch to find the boilers. The school of pollack or the ballan wrasse that live near the boiler are often your first clues that you have reached the site.

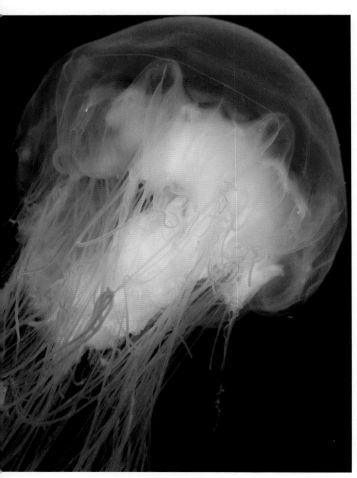

Lion's mane jellyfish

Dive no. 55

Name
Pettico Wick

Location
Situated at the north end of St Abbs head
GPS coordinates N5554.90 W0209.19

Depth
14 metres

Conditions
Easy dive

Access
Shore access
Via road to St Abbs lighthouse (veer left off road 400 metres prior to reaching St Abbs harbour). Divers' car park on left of road. Path in poor state of repair down steep slope to slipway

Diver experience
Ocean diver

Dive site

Pettico Wick is a shallow, sheltered dive site ideal for training dives. It was in fact the site of my first ever dive and looking back at my logbook, I certainly appear to have enjoyed it, even though it was early March and I was in a 3-mm wet suit. I do have vague memories of it being extremely cold when I got back out of the water. This site is sheltered from east and southeasterly winds and is often diveable when the sites at the harbour are affected by a swell. Pettico Wick is therefore an excellent back-up site should the weather be poor. Once you have arrived at the site and navigated the decaying path down to the slipway, it is easy to plan your dive.

Looking northwest out to sea from the slipway, you will see a rock breaking the surface 120 metres from your position. This rock is called Wick Gaut. The seaward side of this rock is where you will experience the best diving at this site. You have the option to partially surface swim out to Wick Gaut or to submerge at the jetty, if there is enough water, and fin out on a compass bearing. In the past I would have conducted a surface-swim but now I tend to submerge at the jetty and fin out on the compass bearing, as there is life hiding on the rocks that make up the seabed just off the jetty. The choice is yours. Just ensure that you stay offshore from the reef on the other side of the bay, as this area is extremely shallow and covered in kelp. There is a prominent rock on the outer edge of this reef and it is here that I would descend if I conducted a surface swim. Descending here, the diver will drop into 10 metres of water. Coarse sand makes up the seafloor, punctuated by large boulders. These are only lightly covered by orange-and-white dead man's fingers, as there is very little tidal movement here. Soon a wall will form and keeping it to your left and following it along will lead you to Wick Gaut. The wall is fantastic. Dead man's fingers cover the wall more densely and schools of small pollack dart along the cliff. Lion's mane jellyfish gently drift along in the green water and lobster are common, hiding under the boulders on the seafloor. The wall is short and soon it is time to turn around and retrace your fin strokes. Making your way back to the southeast, you will soon leave the wall and a weed-covered, boulder-strewn seafloor becomes the norm. It is fairly monotonous but if you look closely, you will have a good chance of seeing angler fish, lumpsuckers and colourful male dragonets. Needless to say, novices and photographers will enjoy this site, which has another nice little feature that can be explored. It lies directly offshore from the jetty in very shallow water. Here you will find the rock called Wheat Stack, with a tunnel cutting right through it. This makes a nice swim-through to finish off the dive and bring you back to the jetty. Refreshed after a great dive, the climb up the crumbling pathway will not feel too bad.

Pettico Wick is a beautiful spot for a picnic or a barbecue. Also worth a visit is the Mire Loch, situated just on the other side of the road from the car park. This is a really pleasant place to go for a walk and observe the topside wildlife, such as mute swans and various species of butterfly.

Dive no. 56

Name
Pettico Wick jetty, northeast to
St Abbs Head

Location
Pettico Wick
GPS coordinates N5554.90
W0209.19

Depth
12–16 metres maximum

Conditions
Superb diving with caves and
gullies to explore. Severe tide if
you travel too far from Pettico
Wick

Diving guillemots at the jetty to St Abb's Head

Access
Shore dive but best dived with
boat cover. Shore access via road to St Abbs lighthouse (veer left off road 400 metres
prior to reaching st abbs harbour). Divers' car park on left of road. Path in poor state
of repair down steep slope to slipway

Diver experience
Sports diver/dive leader

Dive site
Pettico Wick provides nice sheltered diving, ideal for training. If, however, you fancy
some more dramatic and challenging diving, this site can also provide that for you.
There is a trade-off, though, and the price you pay is that you lose the sheltered conditions of the bay and will soon feel the full force of the tide that rips around St Abbs
Head. It is imperative for your safety when completing this dive from the shore that
you are aware of the tide. I would suggest monitoring it closely and not to wait until
you are aware of it pulling you around St Abbs Head, potentially ending at best in an
embarrassing pick-up by a friendly dive boat or at worst a call-out for the lifeboat. I
stress this warning about the tide here because I have experienced it first-hand. My
first dive at the site was superb, with a maximum depth of 12 metres and no tide what-
soever. The second dive was to just less than 16 metres, suggesting that we went a bit
further out this time. At the time I was half the age I am now and twice as fit and I
struggled to lug myself and my camera back through the gullies to the exit point. Both
my buddies and I had roaring headaches by the time we reached the shore, to find
ourselves faced with a climb up a gully, of which I will coment on later. I find myself,

then, in a quandary. I think you should all know about this wonderful under-dived site, but I also want to make you aware of its dangers. I would say that this is a good shore dive but that it is safer if undertaken with boat cover. So what is the diving like that comes with such a health warning? Superb diving can be experienced by leaving the jetty at Pettico Wick and finning northeast towards St Abbs Head. You can also gain access to this site by climbing down the steep gully to the east of the jetty, although this is very hard work and extreme care is needed. Submerge on entering the water from the end of the jetty and immediately you may find the little tunnel to fin through, in the rock known as Wheat Stack, directly offshore of the jetty. Turn right and fin on, following the reef. Initially the dive is similar to Pettico Wick but it improves all the time as depth increases. As you reach the wall which runs out to West Hurker (dive site 57) you will soon note caves housing monstrous lobsters. Wolffish can be found out in the open here, and the rocks and cliffs become smothered in the east coast's trademark covering of orange-and-white dead man's fingers. Gullies are here to be explored as well and there are small fish such as butterfish to be found in the soft corals. Flounders lie on the sandy sea floor next to very large, vibrant, red sunstars. It is fantastic scenic diving. Ballan wrasse are found here too but the most spectacular encounter you can have comes early on in the year, between April and early July, when you may come nose-to-beak with razorbills and guillemots. Watching them leave their trail of silver bubbles in the water is a fantastic spectacle and it was here that I saw it for the first time. At this point you may be in 12 metres of water and it's probably best to turn back for shore at this point. This site is ideal to dive on days when the weather is marginal, with swells from the east or when the dive boats come round to Pettico Wick to escape the fog that can plague the sites at the harbour and the south side of the headland.

I cannot believe we descended and ascended, in full kit, that steep-sided gully to gain access to the site, but we did, so it is possible. The responsibility as to whether it is safe to do so lies with you but, like diving the site from shore, I probably would not attempt this gully for access nowadays. I'm getting too old. I would now enter from the jetty and fin a little further or, better still, would use a boat.

Lumpsucker at **West Hurker**

Dive no. 57

Name
West Hurker, St Abbs

Location
Northwest end of St Abbs Head
GPS coordinates N5555.06 W0208.98

Depth
22 metres maximum on off-shore reef. At cliff, around 16 metres

Conditions
Fantastic scenic dive, including cave and offshore pinnacles

Access
Boat only

Diver experience
Sports diver

Dive site

West Hurker has to be my favourite dive site around St Abbs Head. For me, it has everything a diver could wish for. If you have the chance of one dive in the area, try this site and you won't be disappointed. It is extremely tidal and is therefore a slack water dive. Dive boat skippers such as Peter Gibson are experts at putting you onto this site when the tide is slack. The dive starts behind a rock at the northwesterly extremity of St Abbs Head, just as it makes its turn into Pettico Wick. The dive is in the other direction, and the diver will fin generally towards the east. The dive boat will take you in very close to the rocks where a very narrow channel is the entranceway to this fantastic dive site. Dropping into the water, divers fin through the narrow gap. A beautiful, 2-metre wide, sheer-sided gully, 12 metres deep and 25 metres long, presents itself before you. You could spend a whole dive here, observing the masses of life that fill the gully. Tiny orange plumose anemones make the most vivid splash of colour. In these you will find edible crab, velvet-backed swimming crabs, spider crabs, butterfish and sea urchins. Looking even closer, smaller creatures appear – sea spiders, small prawns and many types of nudibranch. Rounded boulders make up the seafloor here and scorpion fish hunt around them. All this wonderful marine life, coupled with the fin through the stunning sheer-sided gully, makes an amazing start to the dive, but there is far more to see as it continues. As you exit the gully the view opens up, and in around 13 metres of water you can follow the cliff on your right-hand side or explore an off-lying submerged boulder the size of a house on your left. For this dive, though, you follow the wall. I remember the first time I dived this site. Peter's boat *Selkie* could be seen above me in the 15-metre visibility. Peter had told me that he would point the boat's bow to the next feature of this dive site and I noted a seal in the distance giving me a look before lazily gliding away. It was superb.

Continuing your dive, following the cliff face, large car-sized boulders partially make up the sea floor. Kelp and soft corals grow on these boulders and here you can spend some time with groups of ballan wrasse that emerge from the kelp and from underneath the boulders. Octopus are also found here, although with so much marine life for cover it is hard to spot them. After around 50 metres the wall turns 90 degrees to your right and what looks like a gully opens up. Its floor is made up of sand and small boulders and it rises up to the mouth of a cave that cuts back into the cliff for about 10 metres. Bright orange-and-blue squat lobsters line the walls and expertly-camouflaged scorpion fish wait for something to come close enough to eat. Leopard-spotted gobies are common on the floor of the cave and lobsters hide in the recesses. Once, when I was the only diver in here, a large plume of silt erupted deeper inside the cave, which was a bit disconcerting. I hugged the floor of the cave as I edged further in, as I had an idea what I was going to meet and wanted to give it plenty of room. After another few metres the grey seal that I had seen earlier darted over my head. It was a fantastic moment.

To continue the dive, fin straight out of the cave in a basically northerly direction. This is taking you offshore and you will soon feel the tide. Dropping down to around 17 metres, the rocky reef gives way to a sandy seafloor. With luck, and if you have judged it right, you will fin onto a massive fang-shaped pinnacle that rises up 8 metres. It is plastered in marine life. Schools of pollack are found here and lobsters are plentiful. If you don't find the fang immediately, drift east a little way. In good visibility it is easy to find. Gullies run into the sand on the seaward side of the fang and deep-purple dahlia anemones can be found. There are also more octopus out here. Letting the tide push you eastwards, depth increases a little to a maximum of around 22 metres. Huge cracks split the reef, and looking inside these you have a very good chance of finding wolffish. On my last dive here I saw two of these fish in the same cave and I struggled in the tide to get a picture of them.

As if all this scenic action has not been enough for one dive, West Hurker has one final trick up its sleeve: a very small shipwreck. It is an upturned section of wooden hull with metal fittings such as mooring bollards, beside which cod and ling hide. The section of wreckage is only around 7 metres long and is completely encrusted with marine life, so much so that you have to look very closely to make it out at all. I was lucky that I noticed the metal fittings and I surveyed what I had initially taken to be a rock. Peter Gibson thinks that this may be the remains of the *Phoenix*, a small schooner which sank in the area. Check your gauges: if you are low, it's time to surface.

If you have the gas, carry on and enjoy the magnificent marine life which this site has to offer. Sheer-sided gully, cave, fang pinnacle and a wreck: what more could a diver ask for? It is a fantastic dive and not to be missed.

Dive no. 58

Divers surface off the Skelly at Anemone Gullies

Name
Anemone Gullies

Location
Offshore from Skelly Hole, St Abbs
GPS coordinates N5555.06 W0208.98

Depth
14–19 metres

Conditions
Gully diving. Average visibility 10 metres

Access
Boat only

Diver experience

Sports diver/dive leader

Dive site

Starting the dive in Skelly Hole (dive site 59), the diver drops into a fantastic sandy gully, around 12 metres deep. To find Anemone Gullies you need to fin due north, straight offshore out of Skelly Hole. Immediately on leaving this sheltered gully, you will feel the force of the tide. Depending on how fierce the tide is, it may take a little effort to reach the gullies, but it is certainly worth it. Twenty metres from Skelly Hole, rocky fingers of reef form in the coarse gravel seabed. These fingers soon rise around 4 metres tall and form gullies that are fantastic for the diver to fin along, providing shelter from the tide not only for the diver but also for some large fish. Diving here you may be lucky and meet a large ling resting in the calm water. Being such a high-energy site, the walls are covered in orange-and white dead man's fingers and the tops of the ridges between the gullies are topped by dense coverings of plumose anemones. Wolffish are commonly spotted at this site and big edible crabs find plenty of crevices in the gully walls in which to hide. Velvet-backed swimming crabs are extremely common here and fill the vast majority of the holes, apparently taking over. Large dahlia anemones in every imaginable colour can be found on the floors of the gullies, while on close inspection, smaller creatures are noted under the small boulders and in amongst the seaweed and soft corals. Pipe fish abound, as do leopard-spotted gobies, butterfish and the ever-present scorpion fish. These gullies are full of life and are regarded by many divers as the ultimate dive site in St Abbs.

The gullies themselves are around 30 metres long and, at their seaward ends, around 18 metres deep. Once the diver reaches the end of one gully, it is just a case of finning around the tip of the finger of reef and into the next one. Once more out of the shelter of the gully, you will be exposed to the tide and, depending on the direction and strength of the tidal flow, this may influence which way you decide to travel along the reef. The St Abbs skippers will ensure that you are put on the correct side of the reef to enjoy the dive site to its full potential, should there be any severe tidal movement. As you move around the points into the next gully, it is highly likely that you will see some monstrous pollack and coalfish effortlessly holding station in the tide. There are around eight or ten gullies in all, and most are spectacular. If however you grow tired of the one you are exploring you don't have to fin around its end but can simply rise up and fin across the reef for 10 metres or so before dropping back into the next gully. There is one that stands out for me above the rest. It has anemone-covered walls rising up a good 4 metres on either side. The seafloor is coarse clean sand and the base of the walls are undercut, providing shelter for vast amounts of marine life. I think that the real beauty of this site is that you never know what you are going to encounter but it is likely that you will find something big, something unusual or something exciting. Finning further up the main gully, a bowl-shaped recess opens up on the right-hand side. Here you can see a large ship's anchor that helps to distinguish this gully from the others. After perhaps 30 minutes of exploration, the diver will be disappointed to have to tear themselves away from this site but will most likely have experienced a superb dive. To end the dive and avoid being pushed around St Abbs Head, it is advisable to fin back up the gully you are in, returning to the vicinity of Skelly Hole (dive site 59) or the cliffs at the Skelly where some shelter is available. You can send up your delayed surface marker buoy and enjoy the superb marine life in the shallows while you complete your decompression stops. Make sure you don't stow away your cameras just yet, as this close to the Skelly you may be fortunate and experience an encounter with guillemots, puffins and razorbills which will dive down to investigate your silvery exhaust bubbles. A fantastic way to finish off a dive.

Dive no. 59

Nudibranch at Skelly Hole

Name
Skelly Hole wall dive

Location
The Skelly, St Abbs Head
GPS coordinates N5555.06
W0208.98 On the wall.

Depth
12 metres

Conditions
Excellent scenic wall dive.
Average visibility 10 metres

Access
Boat only

Diver experience
Sports diver

Dive site
This is one of the huge St Abbs dives and is a favourite with many divers. This dive is along the north face of the Skelly, a massive pillar of rock that forms the northernmost point of St Abbs Head. To the west of the Skelly is Skelly Hole, a sheltered

gully that cuts back, forming a channel between the Skelly and Floatcar Rock, an impressive sea stack. Early in the season these rocks are covered with razorbills and guillemots and if you can avoid making too much noise, you will have a fantastic chance to dive with them at this site. I like to end the dive in Skelly Hole and I usually ask to be dropped in the water at an extremely narrow cleft near the eastern end of the Skelly. Above the surface this crack is no more than 1 metre wide but as the diver descends into the crack, it broadens out to around 4 metres when the seafloor is reached at a depth of 12 metres. Looking up is amazing, as the kelp-topped walls converge as they near the surface. It is gloomy in here and marine life tends to be limited. Small clusters of dead man's fingers can be seen and hydroids support nudibranchs. The ever-present scorpion fish look for a meal here too. This is a stunning section of the dive. The bottom metre of the walls is devoid of life, as in storms the rounded boulders that make up the seafloor here scour the walls clean. This gully is around 30 metres long and shallows to around 7 metres before large kelp-topped boulders make further exploration difficult.

This is basically leading into the site known as the Barnyard. In the shallower water at the top of this gully, you may experience your first encounter with the guillemots and razorbills, dropping down from the stacks above you to investigate your bubbles. Finning back out of the gully and reaching the end, you may briefly experience the tide. Turn left, keeping the wall on your left-hand side. Soon you will cross a large spur of rock and come to a small amphitheatre. The wall here is covered in life. Anemones of every colour decorate the scene, along with swathes of dead man's fingers and plumose anemones. Large boulders lie just off the wall, forming swim troughs. Large cod and ling hide here and families of ballan wrasse watch you go on your way. In clear blue water, with the sun streaming down, this makes for an amazing sight. The top of the wall is covered in kelp down to around 5 metres. Below this, soft corals take over and it is in amongst these that you have a great chance to find octopus, edible crab and many different types of nudibranchs. This is a very productive site for the photographer. The wall continues for 100 metres or so before another, much broader gully cuts into the wall. This one is Skelly Hole and has a sandy seafloor punctuated by large boulders covered in dead man's fingers. Make sure you check under these boulders as ling, cod and conger eels are commonly seen. You don't have to look too hard for the ballan wrasse and the pollack as they are hiding in plain sight. As the narrow gully is harder to find underwater that is where I choose to start a dive. I end the dive in the shallow sandy gully of Skelly Hole, where I look for the interesting creatures that live in the sand as well as hoping for another visit from the guillemots and razorbills that nest on the walls above this gully.

Red beadlet anemone at Tye's Tunnel

Dive no. 60

Name
Tye's Tunnel

Location
Next gully to the north of the lighthouse and the Craig (dive site 62)
GPS coordinates N5554.98 0208.21

Depth
Tunnel, 9 metres. Reef off point, 20 metres

Conditions
Nice tunnel through headland. Avoid if surge. Best dived at high tide. Average visibility 10 metres

Access
Boat only

Diver experience
Sports diver

Dive site

This site was named after Dave Tye who ran Oban Divers and is said to have found it. Today it makes an extremely exciting dive and is often the diver's first experience of diving in a real tunnel, as opposed to an arch such as Cathedral Rock (dive site 74). The tunnel is around 40 metres long and forms an easy-to-navigate single route through the headland. High tide is the best time to explore Tye's Tunnel. Calm weather is also required for this site and it should be avoided if there is a swell or a surge. Above the surface, the entrances are difficult to find as there is not much to suggest that a large tunnel travels all the way through the headland. I tend to rely on the expertise of the St Abbs skippers to put me right on the site, although when you have dived it once, it becomes easy enough to relocate. The headland through which the tunnel cuts is the first one west from the Lighthouse. Cleaver Rock is off the western end of the tunnel and this puts you in the general area. I personally prefer to start the dive from the eastern end, on the other side of the headland, where all there is above the surface is a narrow crack. Access to the whole tunnel is only available at high tide, as on the east side there is a ridge that rises to just below the surface. I like to start here so that I always descend as I travel through the tunnel. Diving the site this way also means that you won't have to struggle to turn round and retrace your fin strokes if you find that you don't have enough water to exit at the eastern end. As the diver enters the water and moves towards the crack that marks the eastern end of the tunnel, darkness is complete and no opening is visible, because the tunnel immediately drops down a vertical shaft to around 6 metres. Then the tunnel levels off, reaching a maximum depth of around 9 metres. The walls of the tunnel are covered in nudibranchs and hydroids. Beautiful red beadlet anemones are found in large numbers, which I found surprising as I had always associated them with rock pools and very shallow water. They thrive in the darkness, as do the bright orange squat lobsters and velvet-backed swimming crabs, their red eyes looking sinister in the torchlight. Scorpion fish are numerous here too and they must feed on crabs and shrimps as there is little fishlife in the tunnel.

The inside of the tunnel is only around 3 metres in diameter and divers tend to fin through in single file. The tunnel does widen in sections, forming larger chambers. In one chamber there is a window to the surface through which daylight filters down through the water. The bedrock gives way to a seafloor of rounded boulders as you near the western end of the tunnel. Here you pass under a massive boulder that protrudes above the exit. Once outside the tunnel, marine life is a little bland by the high standards of St Abbs and it is not until you fin north to around 17–20 metres that you will start to pick up some magnificent gullies and be once again in the realm of the wolffish. You always have the option to fin back through the tunnel but do not forget that you will only be able to exit at high tide from the eastern exit. Tye's Tunnel is unique in southeast Scotland and any diver who visits the area should certainly aim to dive the site and get it in their logbook.

Dive no. 61

Diver fins between the propeller blades of the Glanmire *wreck*

Name
Glanmire

Location
St Abbs Head
GPS coordinates N5555.22 W0208.24

Depth
35 metres maximum

Conditions
Scenic wreck. Visibility 5–15 metres. Slack water dive only. A rough guide to predicting slack water at this site is 2.5 hours after low and 3 hours after high water at Leith.

Access
Boat only

Diver experience
Experienced sports diver

Dive site
Thick fog reduced visibility on the morning of 25 July 1912 and time was running out for the steamship *Glanmire*. Off course due to the poor conditions, she would very shortly meet her end, smashing into the Black Carr Rocks. Luckily, all her passengers

and crew had time to make shore safely, but the *Glanmire* was doomed. Slipping back off the rocks in the rising tide, the abandoned hulk drifted north around St Abbs Head, before the damage sustained in the collision took its toll and she made the journey down to her final resting place, in 34 metres of water, 300 metres north of St Abbs lighthouse. It must have been a black day for all those involved but now their shipwreck is one of the most colourful in our seas. If they could see her today, even they might appreciate the beauty of the wreck and all the many creatures that have colonised her.

The shotline usually hits bottom just forward of the two big boilers, which are the largest feature of the wreck. A dive can be undertaken just to circumnavigate these and the large engine block that lies just astern of them. In the small gap of around 3 metres in between these structures, huge pollack hang motionless before eventually sauntering very slowly out of your way. Divers certainly no longer spook these fish and very close encounters can be experienced. The engine block itself has lots of hiding places within it, and large ling are frequently sighted. Wolffish used to be a regular sight here but are less so now. Schools of bib do abound, though, and this attractive fish can be found in some numbers in the enclosed spaces of the wreck, under plates and in the engine block. From the engine block, the prop shaft leads to the stern, with broken plates on either side. The stern lies on its starboard side and rises a full 5 metres off the seafloor. A monster lobster was noted living under the prop shaft here. Finning around the stern, you are presented with one of the most dramatic sights that the *Glanmire* offers: the large four-bladed propeller, its blades around 1.5 metres in length, the rudder falling to the seafloor behind. To capture a diver finning through the prop blades makes for an excellent image. Hard on the sand here, the depth is 32 metres. The trip forward takes you back past the stern, and the prop shaft makes a good reference point to guide you back to the engine block, should the visibility be poor. Once back at the engine and boilers, the diver can very happily while away the remaining dive time investigating this area of the wreck and enjoying the fantastic marine life. Keep an eye on the plates lying on the sea floor, and you will often see big ling darting about. Depending on the size of the tides, the slack water period varies between 20 minutes and around 40 minutes. If the window is longer and you are carrying enough gas, you could move on and explore the bow section, but if the tide is starting to run, it's better to ascend and explore this area another day, as the forward section of the wreck is generally a lot flatter and offers the diver less shelter. If you are lucky, though, and the tides are light, you can fin forward over flattened plates completely covered in dead man's fingers. You will occasionally notice the recognisable shape of mooring bollards or a piece of railing but in general the wreck has been completely obscured by the colonising marine life.

On nearing the bow, the hull breaks completely and you may notice a fire hose reel sitting on the sand. The bow section is only a few metres ahead, and in good visibility you will see it rising above you. In the not-too-distant past, five brass portholes remained here, giving the exploring diver a chance to see something a bit special. These, sadly, have all now have been removed and, probably as a result, the bow has now collapsed into the seafloor. Depth is slightly greater here, at 35 metres, and just aft of the break in the bow there is little wreckage. In poorer visibility it's easy to become disorientated. In average conditions, with visibility of 5–10 metres, navigation is fairly straightforward and it doesn't take long to find the debris trail leading back to the main sections of the wreck. On the sand to your right, you will notice a small donkey boiler which is home to an edible crab or two. Take a moment here to look under the plates that lie on the seafloor and you will be rewarded by sightings of ling, conger, or even one of those elusive wolffish, or, if not, a lobster, octopus or even the tiny *Sepia Atlantica*, a small cuttlefish which can be seen over the sand here. The diver will by now have noted that the wreck is home to a great many fish and shellfish of a larger-than-average size, thanks to the fact that the wreck lies in the St Abbs and Eyemouth Voluntary Marine Reserve.

By now the tide will undoubtedly be picking up again. The boilers will now be directly in front of you and the shotline will be visible. If you have delved into the realms of deco stops it will not be long before you experience the tide tugging at your fin tips and in big tides you can feel like a flag on a flagpole as the tide pushes you horizontal. Whatever your underwater interests, the clear visibility, the large sections of impressive wreckage and abundant marine life that inhabits the wreck are sure to impress any diver and leave a lasting impression of the *Glanmire*.

Diver and sunstar at the Craig

Dive no. 62

Name
The Craig

Location
Point directly underneath St Abbs lighthouse
GPS coordinates N5555.22 W0208.24, Hard on the wall

Depth
12–19 metres

Conditions
Wall dive with excellent gullies. Average visibility 7 metres

Access
Boat only

Diver experience
Ocean diver/sports diver

Dive site
The Craig is the headland on which St Abbs lighthouse stands. Diving here starts off shallow, before the diver can venture into deeper gullies. You have a very good chance of witnessing some amazing animal behaviour here, as I have done. Immediately on entering the water and descending, you will note the mouth of a large gully cutting into the cliff.

Depth here is around 10 metres and this sheer-sided gully continues for around 30 metres. Marine life abounds here but it is generally smaller fish such as gobies that are found. Nudibranches are everywhere, from the kelp stalks at the top of the wall, to in amongst the soft corals and anemones that cover the cliff. There are some really nice dahlia anemones to be seen as well. Sea hares are usually a bright red colour and grow to around 10 centimetres and can be seen crawling along the seafloor. Although they are easy to miss even for such a large nudibranch. Once you get your eye in, though, you will notice them quite frequently. Cowries and sea spiders can be seen around the kelp holdfasts. All in all, a lot of marine life to keep novice divers and macro-photographers occupied. This gully ends in a dead end, forming a large concave bowl where lobsters scuttle about on the seafloor. To leave this gully, you will have to fin back to the single entrance. Outside the gully, the wall falls away to 19 metres and finning in a westerly direction will bring you to some great dark gullies to explore. There are some fantastic walls topped by large plumose anemones, and in the gullies' base, bright red sunstars hunt the smaller brittle stars. It is not uncommon to see porpoise on the surface at this site and in 2007, I saw risso's dolphin and minke whales. According to the skipper, the whales were all around me as I was diving, although I never saw them underwater. What I did experience was amazing enough, though, even though I had a macro-lens on my camera and could not capture an image. It was nearing the end of my dive and I was taking an image of a luminous green Devonshire cup-coral when the bright 7-metre visibility turned black. 'Whale!' I thought, and checked around, above and behind me. What I saw was a lot bigger than a minke whale: a massive school of silver herring shimmering a metre away from me, completely obscuring the surface and everything in front of me. Each herring was bigger than I expected, at over 30 centimetres long, and other than the wall at my back, all I could see were herring writhing a metre away from me, the fish at the outer edge of the school trying to get deeper in to avoid the predators which were obviously feeding on it.

I now decided that it was time for me to ascend which, looking back, might not have been one of my best ideas. I sent up my delayed surface marker buoy and finned out into the school from where I hoped to catch a glimpse of the minkes feeding. I hung around at 6 metres with the fish darting on either side of me but I didn't see a whale. I assumed that they would use their sonar and know I was in the school. I knew toothed whales used sonar to hunt but I honestly didn't know if minke whales did the same. I still get the chills when I think about the possiblility of an 8-ton minke bursting out of that school of fish. Recent evidence shows that baleen whales do use sonar for location but that they also have excellent hearing and it was probably my excited bubbles that let the whales know I was there. While nobody can guarantee experiences like that, the deeper gullies of the Craig will be of great interest to the more experienced diver.

Dive no. 63

Big pollak at East Craig Gullies

Name
East Craig gullies

Location
200 metres northeast of the Craig (dive site 62)
GPS coordinates N5554.94
W0208.11

Depth
23 metres

Conditions
Superb deep gullies. Average visibility 10 metres

Access
Boat only

Diver experience
Sports diver/dive leader

Dive site

This is a superb dive site and new to me. Skipper Peter Gibson dropped me onto this site, which is unknown to most divers and located around 200 metres northeast of the Craig (dive site 62), which is the headland with the lighthouse on it. I was dropped into 18 metres of water and a maze of gullies spread in all directions. I followed these gullies as they became ever more impressive, growing wider, their floors becoming sandy. Depth increases to 23 metres where a gully turns a corner and a huge cliff rises up past the extremes of the day's 5-metre visibility. This cliff fronted a sandy seafloor. Marine life is spectacular here and I soon found wolffish hiding in their holes around a metre off the seafloor. Peter had supplied me with a bearing to follow to end up on a reef but I could not bring myself to follow that plan with so many fantastic gullies offering themselves up for exploration. After 25 years of diving this area, it's great to be put onto a new site, and particularly great when it's so good. I will be making tracks to get back to this site and explore it further in better visibility, as the orange-and-white dead man's fingers and plumose anemones which cover the deep gullies will look spectacular in early morning sun.

Dive no. 64

Angler fish at Ealicar Rock

Name
Ealicar Rock to the Craig

Location
Ealicar Rock, St Abbs Head
GPS coordinates N5554.82 W0207.95

Depth
19 metres

Conditions
Low-lying rocky reef. Average visibility 7 metres

Access
Boat only

Diver experience
Ocean diver

Dive site
Paul O'Callaghan, the skipper of the *Lazy G Diver* dropped me onto this site the day after the 2009 St Abbs and Eyemouth Voluntary Marine Reserve Splash-In photographic competition. It will soon be obvious why I remember the date so clearly. It was a site I had never dived before and one that dive boats out of St Abbs tend to steer straight past. I am always willing to take a splash at a new site, so I dropped into the water with a boatload of divers. Descending to the bottom, it was at first a bit of a disappointment. The reef protruded about 30 centimetres above a layer of coarse pebbles

and didn't look too interesting. The instructions given were to fin northwest towards the Craig, the next headland in that direction. Things started to improve slightly as I finned from rock to rock. The reef started to become more pronounced and patches of dead man's fingers started to appear, but it was still very low-key for St Abbs diving. Further north, some more interesting rock formations, about the size of a car, started to appear. Ballan wrasse had set up home around here and more small pollack were to be seen. Depth was around 19 metres at the deepest point and the visibility was reasonably good at 7 metres. Now, walls and ridges started to emerge and the covering of marine life started to reach the standard you would expect from a dive around St Abbs Head. I decided to fin up a gully and, finding a dead end, finned inshore where flat-topped boulders about a metre across formed the seafloor. These had a slight covering of silt as they were lying out of the main tidal stream that rips around St Abbs Head. This looked to me to be ideal angler fish territory and I was desperate to find one. Luck was on my side and, amongst the weed-fringed boulders, I spotted a nice specimen. Of course, it was a day too late, but finding impressive creatures just after an underwater photography competition is generally the norm and I wasn't complaining. At least I did have my camera with me, which I had vowed never to dive without after one too many encounters with angler fish while the camera was still on dry land.

When I returned to the *Lazy G Diver* the other divers were raving about this dive. They had been diving around St Abbs Head all week and they had really enjoyed the change of habitat and the chance to see different types of marine life. If you find yourself in the enviable position of diving St Abbs for a week, do take the chance to complete a dive at this unusual and rarely-dived site.

Black Carr diver and ballan wrasse

Dive no. 65

Name
Black Carr Rocks, St Abbs

Location
Next set of offshore rocks north of Wuddy Rock (dive site 67) GPS coordinates N5554.42 W0207.66

Depth
15 metres

Conditions
Nice wall dive. Average visibility 10 metres

Access
Boat only

Diver experience
Sports diver

Dive site
Black Carr is another of the big dive sites at St Abbs Head, the next set of offshore rocks north of Wuddy Rock. For this dive, we will stay right on the wall of the rock enjoying the superb cliff faces. Maximum depth should be 15 metres. Dropping into the water on the shoreward side of Black Carr, the diver will reach the seafloor around 9 metres down. Coarse sand and boulders make up the seafloor. Even here the walls are spectacular, being completely covered in orange-and-white dead man's fingers. Fishlife is excellent too with wrasse and pollack darting around. Hermit crabs and scorpion fish can be found between the boulders on the seafloor. All this is visible from where you land on the seafloor and the dive only improves as you continue around the wall. Keeping the cliff on your left-hand side, fin along the wall, following it around to the seaward side of the rock. Depth rapidly increases and any traces of kelp are left behind in the shallows, but a dense canopy of it covers the top 5 metres of the walls and, looking up in the often-superb visibility, you will see it swaying above you. Further down the wall, dead man's fingers take over and are so densely packed that there is not room for sea urchins to get a foothold, being relegated instead to the boulders at the base of the cliff. Cracks and crevices are cut into the rock and at a depth of 15 metres, there is a good chance that you will see a wolffish. Mostly though, this is home to lobsters and squat lobsters, and the red-eyed velvet-backed swimming crab is never very far away. With all this shellfish around, it's no wonder that Black Carr is a great place to spot a lesser octopus, and I have been lucky enough to find a few here. On the offshore side of the rock, the walls are truly spectacular, making a beautiful sight in clear water and sunlit conditions. Larger ballan wrasse and schools of pollack also play a part in the scene. After around 150 metres, the wall ends as the northernmost extremity of the rocks is reached, and it's time to turn west and head into shallower water where, once again, the kelp starts to take over.

This dive is a fantastic shallow wall-dive and can be enjoyed by all but real novice divers. For the more experienced diver, another superb dive starts here, called Black Carr Gullies (dive site 66).

Cod at Black Carr Gullies

Name
Black Carr Gullies

Location
150 metres east of Black Carr Rocks
GPS coordinates N5554.42 W0207.66

Depth
15–30 metres

Conditions
Scenic gullies. Average visibility 10 metres

Access
Boat only

Diver experience
Sports diver

Dive site
Black Carr Gullies lie just to the east of Black Carr Rocks (dive site 65). You can be dropped directly onto the gullies if you wish, but I prefer to start the dive on the shoreward side of Black Carr. Rather than completing the wall dive as described in dive site 65, you continue to fin offshore in an easterly direction. A boulder slope gently falls away and depth soon increases to around 18 metres. This is ideal territory for finding wolffish so make sure you look in the holes under the boulders here. Brittle stars take over for a while but fin on past them. At a depth of around 20 metres, the terrain will change and the reef will form overhangs over a nice sandy-floored gully. Turning to your left and keeping the wall on your left, you can fin along the gully with the wall rising and becoming ever more impressive above you. Depth will be around 22–25

metres and it is around here that you will find a large ship's anchor. I wondered if it could be the *Glanmire*'s anchor, as this wreck lies fairly close by (dive site 61) and she ran onto Black Carr Rocks before floating off to sink just to the north. Apart from the anchor, the wall is nice and there are holes in it just off the seafloor. If you find this area, you have an extremely good chance of finding a wolffish. Finning further on, the wall starts to drop back to the seafloor and becomes like a finger pointing into deeper water. Following it down, you will easily find yourself in 30 metres of water. Crossing over the finger of rock and ascending slightly, you will run into a series of gullies which you can explore while making your way back into shallower water. Huge rocks covered in orange-and-white dead man's fingers can be found here and under these you can expect to find ling and cod. Out on the reef itself, there are a lot of butterfish and scorpion fish to be seen, in between the weed and soft corals that cover the boulders here. Nudibranchs are found on the kelp and big edible crabs wedge themselves into cracks and crevices. This is an exciting dive and is slightly deeper than the usual dives completed around St Abbs so do watch your gas supply.

The area of gullies and reef that extends from Black Carr Rocks on the seaward side is expansive and provides many different dive sites. The one I have described is a dive which I like to complete, but don't let that restrict you in your exploration, as the reefs and gullies in this area are superb. If you have good boat cover, it is up to you where you go to explore. I am sure that, whichever way you decide to turn, Black Carr Gullies will provide you with a very nice dive.

Dive no. 67

Name
Wuddy Rock

Location
1 km northeast of St Abbs harbour
GPS coordinates N5553.35
W0207.82

Depth
12–17 metres

Conditions
Tunnels and swim-throughs. Extremely scenic site. Average visibility 10 metres

Wuddy Rock

Access
Boat only

Diver experience
Ocean diver

Dive site
Wuddy Rock is found at the first headland on heading round St Abbs Head from the harbour. It's a shallow site with a maximum depth of around 17 metres, if you stay around the rock itself. Visibility at this site can be spectacular in the summer months, giving you the ability to really appreciate the tunnels and swim-throughs that this site offers for the diver. Entering the water to the south of the rock, the walls of the Wuddy rise up vertically from the sea floor, and in clear visibility the soft-coral encrusted walls can be viewed all the way up to the surface. This can be confusing, as although the walls rise vertically, they cut back on themselves and the uninformed diver may fin straight by this site's best features. That is why the entry from the south is a help, as from this side the two tunnels that run right through the rock are most visible, especially with the sun high at your back. That said, you will have to look hard to find them, even from the south. Finning along the seafloor from the seaward side of the rock with the cliff on your right-hand side, you will come to a rounded buttress of rock completely adorned with dead man's fingers. Finning around this, you will see the wall re-form after a gap. It is this gap which you have to investigate. The more inviting gully here stares you straight in the face but the better tunnel lies up to your right-hand side, although you can't yet see the entrance. Fin up to your right, getting a bit shallower, rise over a big boulder and fin to the back of a short gully. Here, on your left-hand side, is the entrance to the main gully of Wuddy Rock. It's narrow, only 3 metres wide at best, and the walls rise vertically all the way up the 14 metres to the surface. Light streaming in from above silhouettes the kelp which covers the gully roof. The walls are covered in life with dead man's fingers and large swathes of white plumose anemones which may be feeding in the gentle tide which can pull you through the tunnel. Scorpion fish abound on the walls and nudibranchs are visible in the full spectrum of colours. The tunnel is 20 metres long and its walls bell out as they near the seafloor. The walls come very close together, almost meeting at the top but just failing to make it and, in sunny conditions, this lets light shine down into the tunnel.

At the tunnel exit on the north side, you have a choice. By continuing to fin straight out of the exit you will eventually come to Black Carr Rock (dive site 65) and its impressive walls and gullies which are a little deeper at over 20 metres. It's well worth the trip as the Black Carr makes a great dive site. On this dive, however, we want to see the other gully which runs through the Wuddy and this is on your left hand side as you exit the first tunnel. It's not at first obvious, though, as you have to rise over a ridge, following the rock round to your left, before an entrance starts to look promising. This gully rises up and the depth shallows to 6 metres at points. It also opens up somewhat in the middle, where a third gully shoots off to your right, but don't bother going up it. Here you will usually encounter a family of inquisitive and very colourful ballan wrasse. Butterfish also scuttle about between the soft corals. The gully seems to have ended here but there is a narrow crack below you, just wide enough for a diver to get through. Descending it is quite exciting as the dead man's fingers close in on you. You now have to fin along this tight passage, which is just over a metre wide. It once again looks as if the gully has ended, but light is entering from the tunnel mouth below, inviting the diver down, and from here the exit is visible. Here, just to your left, is the little gully which you finned up to get into the first tunnel. The round trip has now been completed.

It's up to you what you do now. If you have enough gas you could do it all again, reverse your route or even take the trip to the Black Carr (dive site 65).

This is a magnificent scenic site that should not be missed. It is certainly one of the best sites that St Abbs has to offer.

Dive no. 68

The Horn ling

Name
The Horn, St Abbs

Location
500 metres directly off St Abbs harbour
GPS coordinates N5554.12 W0207.42

Depth
22 metres

Conditions

Isolated reef, slack water required. Average visibility 7 metres

Access

Boat only

Diver experience

Dive leader

Dive site

The Horn is a narrow ridge of rock, around 200 metres long, that rises 8 metres off the 22-metre deep seafloor. On both sides of the central spine of the ridge, the walls fall away sharply to the floor. The Horn is an isolated site, a massive boulder surrounded by coarse sand. To marine life, the Horn is an oasis, giving shelter where otherwise the sand would give nothing. Life explodes around this site, which is swept by the full force of the St Abbs tidal stream. Larger predators can be found here taking advantage of the abundance of food that the site provides. For the diver, this is an ideal site yet just ten years ago it was unknown. Lying offshore, dive boats took their passengers to see the delights of St Abbs Head, leaving this site undived by the masses. Thankfully that has now changed and the Horn is a popular site, when the tide permits.

Descending down the shotline the diver will note that this site is slightly deeper than the average St Abbs dive. The ridge appears out of the green gloom and the diver decides to fall down the southern side of the ridge, reaching the seafloor in 22 metres. The walls now loom above the diver and they are carpeted in dense coverings of orange-and-white dead man's fingers and plumose anemones. There is some wreckage here but it looks to be disregarded junk rather than the remains of a ship. A small amphitheatre forms on this side of the wall and schools of small pollack dart up the cliff, illuminated in the diver's torchlight. The odd dahlia anemone and large sunstar can be seen out on the sand at the base of the wall. Smaller starfish cover the wall alongside Northern prawn, pipefish, topknot, squat lobsters and two-spot gobies. As the diver fins in an easterly direction, the height of the wall decreases to around 2 metres off the seafloor. Here, large horizontal fissures open up and you can see big cod and ling, around a metre long. They don't move too far away from the diver, secure in their shallow recess. The ling are here to feed on the masses of small pollack and will feed more actively when night falls. The cod will feed on anything but they will target the edible crabs, lobster, flatfish and brittle stars. I would certainly like to complete a night dive here. The ridge eventually peters out completely so the diver can retrace their fin strokes, perhaps taking the opportunity to move over to the more northerly side of the Horn. Its terrain is almost identical, although there are perhaps fewer soft corals. The walls just off the seafloor here are also full of holes and it is here that you are likely to find wolffish. This site has become very popular with photographers and they do well here, whether using close-up or wide-angle lenses, as there is scenery and marine life to accommodate both formats. The diver does need to be aware, though, that the greater depth of this site makes both time and air disappear that little bit faster.

Dive no. 69

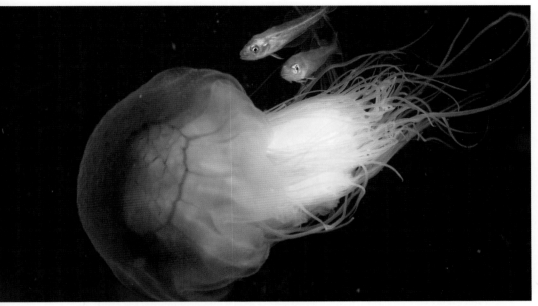

Lion's mane jellyfish and juvenile whiting at Seagull Rock

Name
Seagull Rock (also known as Maw Carr)

Location
St Abbs harbour, directly offshore from the fishermen's car park

Depth
13 metres

Conditions
Easy dive. Average visibility 8 metres

Access
Easy access only if dived at high tide

Diver experience
Ocean diver

Dive site
Seagull Rock is the popular name used by divers for this site, while Maw Carr is the name you will see if ever you look for it on a chart. This is a fantastic dive for all levels of experience, but it is often overlooked by divers who fail to see its potential.

Access to the site is very easy. Park your car in the fishermen's car park and walk into the water. It's as simple as that, at least if you dive around high tide, but make sure you don't try this site an hour after the ebb has started on a spring tide, when the water level drops very quickly. If you stick to these guidelines you can avoid surfacing to find yourself having to clamber over slippery reef and rocks to exit the site, which is fun only for the folk watching from the car park. I used to use the entry point along the old sewage pipe at the north end of the car park but now I find the access ramp on the outside of the seawall makes life very easy. It is just a straightforward snorkel of around 150 metres through the reef to reach Seagull Rock. The water is shallow, at only around 2–4 metres, as you make your way out to the site. Before you even reach Seagull Rock you will have noted shore crab, shannies and beautiful red beadlet anemones. You may even find a lesser-spotted dogfish in the shallow water. This is one of the few sites around St Abbs where I have noted this small British shark. On arriving at Seagull Rock, you will note that the seafloor falls away to 10 metres and is covered with golden sand. Descend here: it is very picturesque with the kelp-topped wall on one side and Seagull Rock on the other. Visibility is generally very good at this site and the sunlight is reflected back off the sand, making a very bright start to the dive. I generally complete the circuit of Seagull Rock in a clockwise direction and keep the wall on my right. Finning along, small gobies and prawns dart out of the sand. Both are on the menu for plaice which I have seen here. Soon, a broad sandy gully leads offshore and it is best to follow this. Schooling pollack are found in this gully and they can be observed feeding on sand eels. Velvet-backed swimming crab and lobsters fill the cracks in the wall, while cowries and nudibranchs are common sights. Just move along the wall slowly, looking for all these tiny creatures, and your eye will soon start to pick them out. Moving further along the gully, depth increases to a maximum of 13 metres and the sand becomes covered by boulders. The gully ends at this point, as the seaward side of Seagull Rock is reached.

It is important that you do not stray too far away from the wall here, as the harbour fairway runs close to the back of Seagull Rock. Following the wall round, a great feature of the site starts to form: a large cave that runs into the rock for about 15 metres. It tapers along its length and at the very back it's a squeeze to get in to look at the scorpion fish, leopard-spotted gobies and Yarrel's blennies that inhabit the darkest recesses of the cave. Squat lobster and velvet-backed swimming crab fill all the nooks and crannies, with the odd edible crab in residence too. Have a good close look at both the walls of the cave, as they are covered in life including fantastically-camouflaged scorpion fish which, although invisible in ambient light, are highlighted bright red in the diver's torch beam. Out of the cave, the dive continues round the rock and soon, another beautiful sandy gully can be explored on the south side of the rock. It is full of lobsters and topknot that hide on the rock ledges and there are some really nice dahlia anemones too. Once you have taken in the sights at this gully, you are basically back at your start point, ready to ascend and glide back to the exit point. Keep your eyes peeled for lion's mane jellyfish with small whiting in amongst their stinging tentacles. Stick to the advice about the tides and Seagull Rock will most likely become another of your favourite St Abbs dives.

Ballan wrasse – one of the UK's most colourful fish

Name
Great Green Carr (also known as Big Green Carr)

Location
St Abbs

Depth
10–17 metres

Conditions
Very nice, easy shore dive.
Average visibility 8 metres

Access
Shore

Diver experience
Novice

Dive site

This site is a fantastic shore dive, perhaps coming second in the popularity stakes behind Cathedral Rock (dive site 74) for the best St Abbs shore dive. There is no issue with finding this site, as the rock around which the dive is completed is clearly visible from the entry point. A short surface swim of around 30 metres will take you to the dive's start point or, if you are confident, you can submerge and fin out on a compass bearing, finning onto the wall. Assuming that a surface swim has been conducted, look down through the water column as you near the rock and when you see kelp below you, descend. I generally dive around this site in a clockwise direction. On descending, you will fall down a magnificent cliff covered in orange-and-white dead man's fingers. The seabed here is of rock and patches of coarse sand, and depth will be around 10 metres at this point, reaching a maximum of 17 metres on the seaward side of the rock. Finning along the cliff, you will immediately note a hole at the base of the wall, home until a few years ago to a friendly wolffish. Sadly, he is no longer there but there is usually something interesting in residence in his place. There are always ballan wrasse around here, and if you are lucky you may have an escort for the first part of your dive.

With the wall on your right-hand side, depth starts to increase and a large undercut forms at the base of the wall. The odd large boulder lies on the sea floor here and do make sure you have a look underneath, as I have often noted large ling living there. Just as you reach the northern end of the wall, a feature known as the chimney comes into view. What starts as a cave narrows down to a swim-through in which you rise up the narrow passage, exiting through a small hole some 4 metres up the wall. I always enjoy this feature of the site. A few years ago, large boulders blocked the exit but I was glad to see on a recent dive that storms had removed them. Now, at the northwestern point of the rock, the depth increases and the wall becomes gentler in its descent to the seafloor. There are lots of scours in the rock carved by the pounding waves and these are now full of life. Lightbulb tunicates and scorpion fish are often to be seen and, if you are lucky, you may spy an octopus hiding between the boulders on the seafloor. It now drops away again and, depending on the tide, you can be as deep as 17 metres here. The walls become vertical again but are much more barren than on the shoreward side, as this wall faces the full might of the North Sea and life is harder here. The seafloor is now sandy so keep an eye out for flatfish. Other reefs and gullies can be viewed offshore from this point, but on this dive we continue to follow the wall around Great Green Carr, where we come to the site's most impressive feature: an amphitheatre rising straight up out of the seafloor. To the right of this feature a large crack runs right up the wall, just a bit too narrow for a diver to enter. In the amphitheatre itself, horizontal cracks have enlarged to sizeable caves which are now home to lots of interesting creatures: leopard-spotted gobies, topknot, Yarrel's blennies and rows of lobsters. If you have a macro-lens on your camera, you will be spoiled for choice. That said, the dramatic scenery of this fantastic dive site is perfect for wide-angle photography too. It's here at the southern end of the amphitheatre that families of ballan wrasse reside, on kelp-topped spurs of rock that lead away from the wall, and if you are lucky you will be inspected by these curious fish. They may have escorted you in, and may well see you out too.

You have now almost completely circumnavigated the rock and after finning through a narrow gully will enter the channel between Great Green Carr and Broad Craig (dive site 72). Here is a sandy-floored cave that is worth a look. Depth is shallowing now and you have to get over a ridge of kelp-lined rock to get back into the main gully on the shoreward side of the rock, from where you started the dive. If gas permits and you have your compass bearing, it's worth finning back to the exit underwater. There are expanses of sand ringed by kelp and boulders and if you run your fingers through the sand, shrimps, dragonets and gobies, almost invisible until they move, will dart about and give you a peek. From here it is just a few metres to the exit point.

Dive no. 71

Name
Little Green Carr

Location
St Abbs harbour

Depth
16 –18 metres

Conditions
Small island with nice walls.
Average visibility 6 metres

Access
Shore or boat access

Diver experience
Sports diver

Velvet-backed swimming crabs at Little Green Carr

Dive site

Little Green Carr is the speck of rock that you can see breaking through the surface behind Broad Craig (dive site 72). It looks a long way out, especially if you surface when you are out there. Realistically, though, you are not much further from the exit point than if you were diving Cathedral Rock (dive site 74) and the sites past that. The water is deeper, though, with general depths of 16–18 metres. Visibility will often be 5–10 metres. There are two ways to reach the rock: you can either fin around the northernmost end of Broad Craig, take a compass bearing and fin out to Little Green Carr, or you can go via the gully between Broad Craig and Scott Rock, as described in dive site 73. Once through the gully, a northeasterly compass bearing will bring you onto the surprisingly large rock that is Little Green Carr. The kelp-covered boulders of the seafloor give way to the walls of the island, which are covered in dead man's fingers and dahlia anemones. There are lots of ballan wrasse and pollack out here too. Breeding pairs of velvet-backed swimming crab peer out from the safety of their hiding places in small caves, or from underneath large boulders, their beady red eyes catching the diver's torchlight. If you feel you have become disorientated on circumnavigating the rock, remember that finning west will bring you back inshore. You should notice the depth decreasing as you come back in. If you don't, carry out a slow ascent to regain your bearings. This is a good site that is rarely visited by divers because of its distance from shore.

Dive no. 72

Name
Broad Craig

Location
St. Abbs harbour, large flat rock opposite entry point

Depth
4–14 metres

Conditions
Easy shore dive. Average visibility 6 metres

Access
Shore dive

Diver experience
Ocean diver

Dive site
This is a simple, shallow shore dive. It's ideal for diver training and it is located right beside the training pool, so can therefore make a great dive for the novice diver after they have completed some training drills. The site can be circumnavigated in either direction. I prefer the anti-clockwise route, keeping the wall on my left-hand side. On leaving the training pool, fin over

Kelp at Broad Craig

the kelp ridge and descend into the gully that leads out to Cathedral Rock (dive site 74). As you descend, look in the cracks and caves on both sides of the gully and you will often see conger eels and wolffish. Pollack and ballan wrasse will come very close to the diver, giving novices a taste of the magnificent diving that can be experienced in the Marine Reserve. When the gully descends into a hole at its deepest point, you have a choice: either take a left turn and fin up into a gully that separates Broad Craig from Scott's Rock (dive site 73) or, if air consumption is looking good, you can fin straight on under an overhang to the end of the gully and follow the wall round to the back of Scott's Rock and Broad Craig. Here, depth increases for a short time to a maximum of 14 metres. The walls, topped with kelp and covered in soft corals, slope more gently here. In between kelp-covered boulders which make up the seafloor are nice, sandy channels where flatfish, shrimps and prawns can be seen. Sometimes large edible crabs rise out of their shallow pits and sand eels can be seen darting in and out of the sand, trying to avoid the attention of the small pollack that school here. As you near the northern end of Broad Craig, depth starts to shallow back to around 8 metres and a broad, flat-bottomed channel forms between this island and Great Green Carr. This is weed-covered and small fish abound here. Velvet-backed swimming crab and vivid orange squat lobsters fill the ledges. These are the favourite prey of octopus and they, too, can be seen here, sitting on the rocks a metre off the bottom, looking at the menu. Turning left again at the end of the northern wall will return you to the training pool and the exit point. This dive is excellent as a taster for the novice diver and will certainly put a smile on their faces. It should not, though, be overlooked by photographers or more experienced divers who may wish to go on and explore part of Great Green Carr (dive site 70) after completing this dive.

Dive no. 73

Leopard-spotted Goby at Scott Rock Gully

Name
Scott Rock Gully

Location
Between Broad Craig and Scott Rock

Depth
4–14 metres

Conditions
A beautiful gully. Calm conditions required, avoid in swell or surge. Average visibility 6 metres

Access

From main gully out to Cathedral Rock (dive site 74)

Diver experience

Sports diver

Dive site

Hundreds of divers fin straight past this dive site, completely unaware of its existence, although this gully, located between Scott Rock and Broad Craig, is easy to find. On making your way out to Cathedral Rock (dive site 74), descend at the corner of Broad Craig and fin down the gully. Soon you will come to a hole, before the gully shallows again and the overhang is noted. This hole is where you need to turn left and rise up a little kelp-covered wall. Initially the gully is only around 8 metres deep and the walls rise only 2 metres on either side. Those walls, though, are very colourful and are covered with orange-and-white dead man's fingers, kelp and redweed. Lobsters, ling and topknot fill the ledges on the right-hand side of the gully. Ballan wrasse reside here and it won't take long before you have a friend to guide you through the gully. The gully gets deeper all the time and the walls become taller and more impressive, reaching a maximum depth of 14 metres. At the seaward end, kelp-covered boulders can be seen along with sandy patches on the seafloor. Here you have the option to turn left and follow the wall around Broad Craig, or to turn right to explore Scott Rock. You can also decide to fin offshore to find Little Green Carr. Be aware, though, that once you leave the seaward side of the gully, depth increases to around 18 metres and it is very difficult to regain entry to the gully, as its entrance is obscured from view by the kelp-covered boulders. This is a small site but once you know it's there, it's easy to incorporate into your dives. One word of advice, though: if there is a swell or surge, this gully should be avoided.

Dive no. 74

Cathedral Rock ballan wrasse with the cathedral in the background

Name
Cathedral Rock

Location
St Abbs

Depth
12–14 metres

Conditions
Always some tidal movement which can be strong in the archway due to the funnelling effect. On spring tides, exploration further out from the archway can be difficult. To complete the suggested dive, good air management will be required. Average visibility 7 metres

Access
Shore

Diver experience
Ocean diver

Dive site
Cathedral Rock is without a doubt the best scenic shore dive I have ever undertaken in the UK. To find this site, enter the water at the end of the harbour opposite Broad Craig (dive site 72). Surface-swim over the training area, which is a large patch of sand. This takes the diver to the edge of Broad Craig. Passing over a ridge of kelp and looking down through the water, the diver will see the start of the gully that leads most of the way to Cathedral Rock. Submerge and follow this gully out southeast, past Broad Craig and Scott Rock, generally on a compass bearing of 120 degrees. There is a depression here before the gully continues under an overhang. This distinctive feature

will help fix your position on your return journey. At the end of the gully, continue to fin out straight on the compass bearing for around another 30 metres. If the depth is greater than 13 metres, you are too far east. You should find a large reef blocking your path. If you move to the left, the reef will end in a series of angular juts, as if somebody has cut steps into the rock with a saw. It's a distinctive feature and again I use it to fix my position. Fin through the gap and Cathedral Rock is now only 10 metres away, although you may not see the arch due to the visibility or the angle of the sun. Veer 45 degrees to your right and after 10 metres you will fin into Cathedral Rock. Large twin arches greet the diver, funnelling the tide through the small island known as Thistley Brigs. Marine life explodes with colour in these perfect conditions. Colonies of ballan wrasse have made themselves a home at the arches and you will know when you are getting close, as they will come out to meet you. A large school of pollack also lives in the lower arch, possibly a couple of hundred of them hanging motionless in the tide, gently parting as the diver fins through them. I have also seen massive cod in the smaller top arch. There is a recess on the west side here and something big is usually to be found hiding in there. A large conger eel has recently taken up residence. As well as the large numbers of fish, the arches are home to lobster, squat lobster, edible crabs and gobies, and on one occasion I was lucky enough to be followed around the archways by a young grey seal pup. The arches are completely encrusted in orange-and-white plumose anemones, well-fed in the tide generated by the arches. The roof of the lower arch is covered in large mussels. These in turn provide cover for scorpion fish and butter fish. At the southeast end of the lower arch is a large flat-topped rock, which I always refer to as the Altar. In the breeding season between May and July, ballan wrasse use it to mate and deposit their eggs there. At that time of year you can generally get even closer than usual to these gregarious fish. The Altar is also covered in hydroids and small anemones. It's an excellent place to look for and spot tiny nudibranchs, although you will have to look closely as most of these sea slugs are less than 2 cm long.

This site should not be missed. It is stunningly beautiful and I find that hovering in the top arch, viewing all the fish going about their business below, is one of my most relaxing experiences. You should give it a go. I do not know for sure how this site gained its name but I do think that a diver entering the archways, no matter how many times they have dived the site before, will feel something spiritual. It may be, though, that it was simply named for its cavernous size and for the Altar at its southeast end.

To get back to the exit point at the harbour, fin from the northernmost side of the arches back to the reef with the angular juts. Then take your reciprocal bearing of 120 degrees. This will take you back to the gully. This is where it gets tricky, though, as there are a few similar gullies here. If you end up in a gully with a floor of rounded pebbles, you need to turn around and follow the easternmost wall round into the next gully offshore. The seafloor here should resemble that of the gully from where you finned earlier. Soon you will come to the overhang which will fix your location. Now just fin back up the rest of the gully but do keep your eyes peeled as there is the chance of seeing wolffish and conger eels among the boulders here. When you emerge from the gully, assuming that you have enough air, drop into the sandy training pool. It's a great place to spot shrimps, hermit crabs and nudibranchs. Surfacing from here your exit point is only a few metres away.

Dive no. 75

Name
Don's Bum

Location
South of Cathedral Rock (dive site 74)

Depth
15 metres

Conditions
Some tidal movement, small tunnel, average visibility 10 metres

Access
Same access as for Cathedral Rock

Diver experience
Sports diver

Dive site
Cathedral Rock (dive site 74) is without doubt the best shore dive in the area. Once you become confident about finding the Cathedral, you will realise that it is surrounded by more fantastic dive sites and you will

Walls of Din's Bum covered in dead man's fingers

want to explore them. To do this safely from the shore, you must be aware of the tide, as the more exposed sites around Cathedral Rock can become difficult to navigate when there is a big spring tide running. If you plan to dive Don's Bum, avoid the spring tides and you should be fine.

I first learnt about Don's Bum from a local diver called Don and he may have something to do with the origin of the site's name. On first diving the site, I was amazed both by the gully and the marine life. Since then it has been a favourite dive which I undertake whenever I have the opportunity.

To find the site from Cathedral Rock, fin out of the southeast end of the arch, staying close to the left-hand wall. Follow this until it starts to turn away to the left. You should turn right here, finning away from the wall. Almost immediately a reef will rise up on your right with a wall rising about 6 metres above you. Follow this wall for around 15 metres. The seafloor here is made of large rounded boulders and is a good place to find angler fish. Soon, the wall on your right peters out, but keep finning in the same direction and you will immediately see a large wall forming on your left. You are almost at Don's Bum: all you have to do is to fin around 15 metres and then a gap will be noted in the wall. On the far side of the gap is a 3-metre drop into the most spectacular sandy gully. It is around 5 metres wide and the walls on both sides rise up to just below the surface. Depth here is 13–15 metres, depending on the tide. All the marine life you might expect to see can be found here. The walls are covered in fantastic colonies of orange-and-white dead man's fingers and plumose anemones that feed well when the tide runs. Large pollack cruise about in gangs and families of ballan wrasse are to be found in the recesses in the walls. Small caves, cracks and crevices form in those walls, full of squat lobster, velvet-backed swimming crab and leopard-spotted gobies. The flatfish known as topknot are often found here, preferring to lie on the rocky ledges rather than the sand where you would expect to find flatfish.

This gully is around 30 metres long but to complete this dive you only need explore half that length. Soon you will notice a fantastic buttress of rock on your left and another magnificent gully runs off at right angles to the one where you are finning. For now, ignore that gully and concentrate on the right-hand wall where you will find a small cave. It's full of that same rich marine life but also often has a huge lobster as a resident. On coming out of the cave, you will see, directly opposite you on the left-hand wall, a dark hole. This is Don's Bum. Entering this hole you will find that it is a small, curved tunnel that takes you into the other beautiful gully which you ignored earlier. The walls are massive, and in bright conditions these gullies are stunning. On exiting the tunnel, fin to your right down the gully, which is also around 30 metres long. At the end of this gully the sandy seabed disappears, to be replaced once again by the seafloor of large round boulders. This is hardly surprising as you have navigated around 3 sides of a submerged rectangular rock. Keep the reef wall on your left and fin along the final wall of the rock. At its end you should remember the point which you have already finned past just before the first gully formed. To get back to Cathedral Rock, turn to your right at the end of the wall and you will soon pick up the 6-metre high reef on the other side of the large boulder field, where you can look for angler fish again. Once this reef disappears from your left and a wall appears in front of you, turn left and you will have completed an underwater circuit back into the rear entrance of Cathedral Rock. From here you can enjoy further gullies all the way back into the exit point but none are as dramatic as the two you have just enjoyed at Don's Bum.

Dive no. 76

Nudibranch on red weed at Ebb Carrs

Name
Ebb Carrs

Location
500 metres southeast of St
Abbs harbour
GPS coordinates N5653.79
W0207.42

Depth
16 metres

Conditions
Superb scenic gully diving.
Average visibility 8 metres

Access
Boat only. Slack water dive only

Diver experience
Sports diver

Dive site
The Ebb Carrs and the *Alfred Erlandsen* (dive site 77) must be one of the most under-rated dive site at St Abbs, even though it is only 500 metres from the harbour. Perhaps that is why: it is just too close to shore to be taken as a serious dive, especially when the majestic headland and spectacular diving of St Abbs Head beckon. I cannot stress too strongly that this site should not be missed, as it is spectacular in terms of its marine life, the terrain of the site and, of course, interesting wreckage in the form of the remains of the *Alfred Erlandsen*. There is even another wreck here called the *Vigilant*, which was a more modern fishing trawler. Ebb Carrs is a large pinnacle of rock rising from 16 metres and breaking the surface only at low tide. This central pinnacle is surrounded by gullies and reefs, and is very similar to the Hurkers dive site off Eyemouth (dive site 86). This is hardly surprising, as a subterranean reef connects the two, Ebb Carrs being the northernmost extremity while the Hurkers are the southernmost point.

Peter Gibson, skipper of the dive boat *Selkie*, took me out to the site. I dropped down straight into a scenic gully. The tides surge around these rocks and the marine life reflects this, with dense coverings of dead man's fingers and plumose anemones. Narrow kelp-topped gullies shelter vast schools of coalfish which will eventually move out of the way as divers fin through their school. Groups of the biggest ballan wrasse I have ever seen are also found here. The cracks and crevices are filled with edible crabs and lobster and more and more velvet-backed swimming crabs now seem to fill the holes. Like pipefish, they have experienced a population explosion over the last few years, perhaps due to the warming of our seas by climate change. Nudibranchs are common and they look fantastic, crawling over the redweed that covers part of the gullies' walls. You may also come across a Yarrel's blenny. Seeing all this magnificent marine life marks the site as a top dive, but when the colourful remains of the *Alfred Erlandsen* are seen, it gets even better. If the tides are right and the skipper of a St Abbs dive boat tells you that the Ebb Carrs can be dived, do not miss the opportunity. You will not be disappointed.

Dive no. 77

Diver investigates the propeller of the Alfred Erlandsen

Name
Alfred Erlandsen

Location
Ebb Carrs
GPS coordinates N5653.79 W0207.42

Depth
16 metres

Conditions
Superb broken shipwreck lying in scenic gully. Average visibility 8 metres

Access
Boat only

Diver experience
Sports diver/dive leader

Dive site
George Colven was, until a few years back, the St Abbs harbourmaster. He was only seven when the *Alfred Erlandsen* went up on the rocks. Just over one hundred years ago, his grandfather's words, "There's a ship ashore!" soon had George and his grandfather running to the cliffs. There was a dense fog and the surf could be heard but not seen, banging and crashing against the rocks. Strangely, though, even though the sea was wild, there was no wind and the night was still. The stricken *Alfred Erlandsen* had run onto the treacherous Ebb Carrs, just 500 metres southeast of the harbour, at half past eight on the evening of 17 October 1907. The ship's steam whistle and intermittent shouts of her men could be heard periodically above the noise of the surf. Then, at nine o'clock, the fog temporarily lifted, giving the gathered villagers and George a fleeting glimpse of the horror that was unfolding less than half a mile from shelter and safety. Now the telephone was used to call for help. A three-pronged rescue plan was put into action. The Eyemouth and Skateraw lifeboats were launched, and a heavy horse-drawn cart thundered along the muddy road from Eyemouth to St Abbs, carrying lifesaving apparatus. It stopped at Castle Rock Villa, the nearest point of land to the wreck. The rescue party fired eight rockets in all but none made it near the wreck. By now, the tinkling of the ship's bell and the sounding of the steam whistle had stopped, and there were no more sounds from the crew. Now only the sound of shrieking metal, tearing on the rocks, vied with the sound of the crashing surf. It was at this time that George's grandfather told him he'd 'better get in out of the cold'. Launching at half past ten that night, the Eyemouth lifeboat arrived at the scene between eleven o'clock and midnight The sea was running high and the waves were breaking over the deck and funnel of the *Alfred Erlandsen*. The Eyemouth boat made a circuit of the wreck, an extremely dangerous manoeuvre, as the ship's cargo of pit props and timber was loose in the sea. There were no signs of life from the wreck and the Eyemouth boat returned to harbour at two the following morning. The Skateraw lifeboat was battling the mountainous northeastern seas, covering the 20 miles to the wrecksite and arriving at between 2 o'clock and 3 o'clock in the morning. The spilled cargo of timber was smashing against the lifeboat's hull in a most dangerous fashion, but they stood to for an hour at the site. They did not retire from the wreck until permission was received from shore. Then the 15 man crew, 14 at the oars, made the run home on what would be an exhausting round trip of 10 hours in terrifying conditions.

Dawn saw the *Alfred Erlandsen* completely smashed on the rocks. Three bodies were found, two men and a woman, the wife of the master mariner. There was, though, one survivor from the wreck, found guarding the body of a drowned sailor the next morning. A Great Dane, it was christened Carro after the Carr Rocks and found a good home in St Abbs.

St Abbs at the time of the disaster was seeking a lifeboat of its own and while the sinking did not bring immediate results, it certainly added weight to the villagers' argument.

Diving the wreck of the *Alfred Erlandsen* is a fantastic experience. Peter Gibson, skipper of the dive boat *Selkie*, dropped me straight on to the site, and the first piece of wreckage I encountered was a large intact boiler that sits in the middle of a beautiful scenic gully. Check out its rusty holes and you will find scorpion fish, squat lobsters and blennies all over it. Further up the gully, winches and plates lie strewn over the seafloor and mooring bollards sit in the kelp. Rising up the gully all the time, the second boiler is found, this one ruptured so that all the inner piping can be seen. It's home to big pollack and cod and completely covered in soft corals, it really is a lovely sight. This boiler sits on top of a ridge and here the gully restarts its decent to the seafloor. There are more broken plates and fittings here and a large winch guards the mouth of this gully. Finning around into the next gully, the diver will discover the *Alfred Erlandsen*'s large four-bladed prop. This dive has got it all: beautiful scenic gullies with a shipwreck and masses of marine life. I would go as far as to say that this is a better dive than the *Glanmire* (dive site 61) which is regarded as the main wreck site at St Abbs. When you next visit the area, check out Ebb Carrs and see what you think. I think the crew and the wreck of the *Alfred Erlandsen* have found a lovely resting place.

Over the 100 years since the sinking, the gravestone and memorial to the crew has weathered away and the text is almost unintelligible. Local people have raised funds and erected a granite slab as a new memorial to the crew.

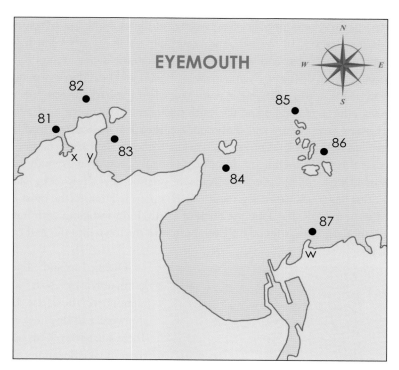

EYEMOUTH

w – access for dive 87 Green Ends Gully
x – Entries/Exits & parking area
y – Exit at Little Leeds bay

Eyemouth

Eyemouth was for a long time the silent partner of the St Abbs and Eyemouth Voluntary Marine Reserve. In the past, the beautifully scenic St Abbs has had better facilities and tended to get more attention, even though the diving around Eyemouth is just as good. Shore diving at Eyemouth was difficult and boat diving was not commercially available until around eight years ago, when the harbour was redeveloped, but since then the large building on the south side of the harbour has been adapted to house Aquastars Dive Centre and washroom facilities. The main driver in this diving renaissance has been Marine Quest, based at the harbour. Their enthusiasm for finding new dive sites and travelling to distant ones on excellent, diver-friendly boats has been rewarded with the discovery of dozens of pristine new shipwrecks and scenic dive sites. This has transformed Eyemouth from a poor relation to the most exciting place to dive in the UK, let alone the Firth of Forth. I am watching with interest to see if the impressive wrecks found off Eyemouth turn the town into the 21st century's Scapa Flow.

Eyemouth harbour

Diving around Eyemouth is mainly by boat and, as mentioned, there are fantastic shipwrecks to dive just offshore. There are, however, two excellent shore-diving locations that are well worth visiting.

Eyemouth is a reasonably large town built up around its large modern harbour, home to the port's large fishing fleet. Eyemouth has a good selection of bars and restaurants, there is a caravan park and a selection of bed and breakfasts and most of the facilities you will require can be found in the town. Travel time to Edinburgh is around an hour.

Dive no. 78

Leager Buss pipe fish

Name

Leager Buss

Location

500 metres off Coldingham Bay, between Eyemouth and St Abbs
GPS coordinates N5553.14 W0207.08

Depth

15 metres maximum

Conditions

Rock pinnacles on sandy sea floor. Average visibility 6 metres

Access

Boat only

Diver experience

Ocean diver

Dive site

I was first dropped onto this incredibly scenic site two years ago. It was a new site found by Jim and Iain Easingwood of Marine Quest. Clean golden sand surrounds the reef which is made up of five or six large boulders. They rise out of the sand and stand a good 5–7 metres off the seafloor, which is reached at 15 metres. Sandy gullies are formed between the rocks, offering a home to many tiny creatures. On my last dive here the visibility was poor and I was running my fingers through the sand. Out popped a tiny lesser weaver fish, the first I had ever seen in the UK. These fish have highly venomous dorsal spines and whilst they dart away well before fingers can get too close to them, I did from then on exercise a little more caution. More juvenile fish appeared out of the sand, some of which I could only take an educated guess at identifying, but this suggests that this site is important for very young fish. The usual larger creatures can be found here too. Kelp covers the top of the boulders and a patchy covering of dead man's fingers forms on the more exposed rocks. There is not a lot of water movement and the coverings of soft corals are limited. Painted topshells, edible crab and velvet-backed swimming crab are all common. There are sea urchins here, and beautiful starfish in purples and orange decorate the walls. Nudibranchs abound, feeding on hydroids, and they can be seen both on the kelp and gliding along the walls. One of their egg ribbons will often alert the diver to their presence, as the egg mass can be much larger than the nudibranchs themselves. Pipefish are also common amongst the weed on the seafloor and there are always schools of small pollack darting about. I would also expect to find angler fish and octopus here, as the terrain looks as if it would suit these creatures, but as yet I haven't noted any.

Leager Buss is therefore an ideal location for the second or third dive of the day. With its flat sandy seafloor stretching away in all directions and a general depth of 15 metres, this site also makes an ideal place to perform more advanced training which requires this depth.

Dive no. 79

Dahlia anemone at Fold Buss

Name
Fold Buss

Location
Offshore, 0.5 miles from Eyemouth

GPS coordinates N5553.13 W0205.40

Depth
27 metres

Conditions
Steep-sided reef. Average visibility 8 metres

Access
Boat only

Diver experience
Sports diver/dive leader

Dive site
Fold Buss is one of the pinnacles that rise up off the reef that runs from the Hurkers off Eyemouth to the Ebb Carrs off St Abbs Harbour. There are a few similar sites along this reef and Fold Buss is probably the best known of them. Being around 0.5 miles offshore, this is an extremely tidal dive site. The wall drops on average from 22 metres to the seafloor at 27 metres. Coarse sand abuts the wall, which makes for a dazzling sight on a sunny day. Wolffish are extremely common here and this must be one of the best places in the area to find them. It is not unusual to see three or four of them on a single dive. Large dahlia anemones in vivid colours line the floors of sandy gullies that cut back into the wall. It is in one of these gullies that the diver will discover a large ship's anchor wedged into the reef. If you plan to dive this site, agree with your skipper that you will be on site for slack water or else diving on a very small neap tide. Attempting this site at other times really does leave you at the mercy of the tide and liable to be washed off the reef. Catch this site just right, though, and you will enjoy a great dive surrounded by magnificent marine life. This dive site does lie near the harbour fairway, so be aware of boat traffic and make sure that you have excellent boat cover.

Painted top shell at Podley Peaks

Dive no. 80

Name
Podley Peaks

Location
Off Eyemouth
GPS coordinates N5553.78
W0205.73

Depth
24–36 metres

Conditions
Underwater pinnacle. Average visibility 6 metres

Access
Boat only

Diver experience
Sports diver/dive leader

Dive site
Podley Peaks is another site that, as far as I know, has never been dived before. It is a submarine pinnacle, rising up from a seafloor which is around 36 metres deep. Jim Easingwood of Marine Quest first placed me onto the site to see what it was like. He had taken parties of anglers to fish over it and they had made many fine catches, so it sounded very promising. This is a similar site to Fold Buss (dive site 79) and forms part of the same underwater reef that runs from the Hurkers at Eyemouth (dive site 86) to the Ebb Carrs off St Abbs Harbour (dive site 76). On the dive, a wall does form but it falls for only 4 metres before a slope of large boulders continues into the depths. These were covered with large dahlia anemones, and their spectacular colours were the highlight for me on this dive. Whilst the anglers may have experienced spectacular fishing, all I noted on the dive were small gobies, although I must admit the terrain looks superb for wolffish and conger eels, and am fairly sure that they could be found at this site. What I did manage to find was anchor chain, and lots of it. I followed the large links of chain down to 36 metres. I was using a single 12-litre tank and pony cylinder for this dive and was already into decompression, so had to abort my search, as the chain was leading deeper down the boulder slope. I wondered if this submerged reef had claimed another ship's anchor. Looking at the amount of chain on the reef, there's a good chance that it had, so keep a look out for it when on the dive.

Dive no. 81

Cave near Diver's Hole at Weasel Loch

Name
Weasel Loch

Location
500 metres northeast of
Eyemouth harbour

Depth
16 metres

Conditions
Excellent dive site, tide can be
strong when out of weasel loch
and onto reef. Average visibility
8 metres

Access

Shore access via caravan park (£3 parking fee) or, more comfortably, by boat

Diver experience

Ocean diver

Dive site

Weasel Loch is a majestic place and is Eyemouth's premier shore-diving site. This is an inlet with 20-metre cliffs on either side of a 7-metre wide gully, which reaches inshore for 100 metres, where it ends in a bowl-shaped lagoon. To access the site from shore, travel through the Eyemouth Holiday Park, situated on the cliffs to the north of Eyemouth Bay. Access from here is by a well-constructed stairway. To park at Weasel Loch, you will need to purchase a parking permit (£3 at present) from reception. Boat-diving at this site makes life a lot easier. You can drop over the side into the 6-metre deep gully onto the clean sandy sea floor with no need to recover from a steep descent of the stairs. Down on the sand, flounders abound, along with shrimps and sand eels, but if you are really lucky you will come across *Sepiola Atlantica*, a tiny cuttlefish. The walls rise vertically on either side of the gully and as you swim offshore, there is a cave on your left-hand side. It's usually full of squat lobsters and leopard-spotted gobies and as this site is in the Marine Reserve, there are loads of lobsters about too. Now, at the seaward end of the gully that forms Weasel Loch, the diver simply turns right and dives along the cliff face. Depth soon increases to 15 metres and the wall is vertical and heavily undercut at its base. This is where you usually find the star performer on your dive. A few years ago it was George, a friendly and very large wolffish, who used to dart out to say hello, frightening the living daylights out of divers who were not prepared to meet him. When he disappeared, a very large lobster moved in and took up residence, but he, sadly, was removed by a diver. Most recently, a very large conger eel has been found here, so do make sure you have a good look in the openings at the base of the cliff, as this is where the big stuff tends to hang out.

Just after these openings, a spur of rock, some 2 metres high, sticks out at right angles to the cliff face. This is an important landmark as it is the gateway to Conger Reef (dive site 82). Deciding to continue diving Weasel Loch, fin over the spur and soon the wall ends, with a large scour in the sand. Depth here can be 17 metres. This is Diver's Hole, another gully that cuts back into the cliff face. In poorer visibility you may not realize that it is 5 metres wide and that the cliff reforms on the far side of the gully. Before you fin over, though, take a good look at the cliff wall where it turns into the gully. Marine life explodes here due to the water movement past this point. Devonshire cup-corals and nudibranchs are found amongst the hydroids here. You can fin up the gully but be aware that you will only be able to exit into Little Leeds Bay (dive site 83) at high tide. If there is any surge in the water, you will not want to be caught up this gully. I generally fin across the mouth of the gully, dragging my fingers through the sand and watching all the shrimps and flatfish darting for cover. Immediately on the far side of the gully, the sand piles up and there is a small cave to explore. This is the last major feature of the dive and the depth shallows from here as you ascend into Little Leeds Bay and relish the climb back up the cliffs, without, I might add, the aid of a stairway. You can always aim to end your dive back at Weasel Loch or, of course, get back into a boat.

One word of warning about this site: it is popular with anglers and there is a lot of their tackle lying around. Make sure you have a knife or line cutter to free yourself should you become entangled.

Dive no. 82

Diver and edible crab at Conger Reef

Name
Conger Reef including the Cresta Run

Location
Offshore, between Weasel Loch and Diver's Hole

Depth
18 metres maximum

Conditions
Amazing gullies. Average visibility 10 metres

Access

Continuation of Weasel Loch shore dive (dive site 81) or by boat

Diver experience

Sports diver

Dive site

For me, this dive site was shrouded in mystery and difficult to locate. For some years I had tried to find Conger Reef and the amazing Cresta Run. Eventually I hit upon a simple way of finding them both. If you read my section on Weasel Loch (dive site 81), the entry point and dives are identical until the diver comes to a spur of rock pointing directly out to sea. This is found just after the overhang at the base of the big wall. Follow the spur offshore and rise over a banked reef covered in kelp and seaweed. Drop down the seaward side of this reef into 18 metres of water. In front of you, you will see two massive house-sized boulders, one to your left and one to your right, with a gully forming a route through to their far side. Before you investigate this, though, look directly to your left and you will note a very narrow gully opening up. This is the Cresta Run, an amazing site often missed by divers who make it out as far as Conger Reef. Fin up this narrow gully: it's only 2 metres wide and both sides rise up 6 metres above you. The gully twists and turns before emerging in the kelp at its western end. There is no grand entrance here and it's easy to see how divers miss this entry point. If your gas is low, you can fin inshore (south) from here and rejoin the main wall, to exit at Weasel Loch. If you have the gas, though, turn round and descend back along the Cresta Run, enjoying the prolific marine life. It's not overly tidal here, so you will mainly see dead man's fingers sparsely covering the walls, with big edible crabs living in the crevices. Schools of small pollack dart around in the kelp that adorns the top of the walls. This is fantastic diving! Once you reach the northeastern end of the Cresta Run, turn left into the gully between the two big boulders that form Conger Reef. There is more water movement out here and the coverings of dead man's fingers are denser. The huge walls rise up a full 10 metres, stopping just 8 metres below the surface. Continuing on the dive, you can choose whether you want to explore the left-hand or the right-hand boulder. It's all exciting diving but it is easy to lose your bearings, so remember that you need to fin south to pick up the main wall. The choice is yours as to which boulder to explore, but I usually fin round the back of the right-hand boulder, keeping the cliff on my right-hand side. There is a further large boulder here to be explored and then a patch of sand develops. Fin on and you will enter Diver's Hole. You can then exit in Little Leeds Bay (dive site 83) as described in the Weasel Loch dive or, even better, get picked up in a dive boat. Having boat cover for this dive really allows you to explore the site thoroughly without the fear of getting lost, especially if you are new to it. Once again, be aware of anglers at this site as there is a lot of discarded fishing tackle. You really do not want to be caught hook, line and sinker so make sure you have a dive knife or a line cutter to be on the safe side.

Dive no. 83

Little Leeds Bay shore crab

Name
Little Leeds Bay

Location
Next bay east from Weasel Loch (dive site 81)

Depth
9 metres

Conditions
Very shallow dive. Average visibility 6 metres

Access
Shore access from car park at caravan park (£3 parking fee)

Diver experience
Ocean diver

Dive site
Most divers will think of Little Leeds Bay as merely the exit point from a dive around the headland from Weasel Loch (dive site 81) and I tend to agree with this way of thinking. I would not bother to descend the rocky path down the cliff to dive this site

unless I had very good reason. The site is excellent, though, for diver training and for some this will be reason enough. Once the diver gets past the kelp-covered boulders, a sand-and-gravel seafloor takes over at around 9 metres. At this depth there are some large boulders that are interesting to look under. There is no shortage of marine life to look at: two-spot gobies, painted topshells and most types of crab can be found here. There is a little swim-through to be found near the centre of the bay, almost in line with the back of Diver's Hole. This site is somewhat protected from northerly and westerly winds, and this is when this site does come into its own. There are just too many good sites to explore, and even better training areas, where the entry is much less stressful and does not include a descent down a steep path. Weasel Loch, found just to the west, makes an easier alternative. It has a solid stairway down to the water and the sandy floor of that site is 6–9 metres deep. That site, however, is susceptible to northerly winds. For the best diving conditions in Little Leeds Bay, I would suggest diving at high tide, making access and egress over the shallow kelp-covered boulders much easier.

Dive no. 84

Bright red scorpion fish at Fort Point

Name
Fort Point

Location
Beneath the headland on north side of Eyemouth bay, immediately out of Eyemouth harbour

Depth
15 metres

Conditions
Surprisingly good diving. Scenic gullies. Average visibility 7 metres

Access
Boat only

Diver experience
Ocean diver

Dive site
I had sailed past Fort Point on many an occasion but had never dived it. It is right outside Eyemouth Harbour, on the

left-hand side as you look out to sea, and does tend to get overlooked. Don't be put off by its proximity to the harbour as this is a spectacular dive. Descending into 10 metres of water on the shoreward side of the islet Luff Hard, you will enter a maze of gullies penetrating the reef walls and taking you through to the outside face of the reef. This site is also just across the bay from the River Eye and I have seen a large salmon here, waiting its turn to fin up the river to spawn. It was in an exhausted state but swam close to me a few times before buzzing me and veering away at the last moment. This was a first and memorable experience for me, but Fort Point has many more features to excite the diver. Head on through one of the three narrow gullies that lead to the outer reef. One gully is very narrow and I have seen a tree trapped on the sea floor here. Divers will marvel at the coverings of soft corals that cover the walls, as they reach all the way up to the surface. Fronds of kelp enclose the top of the gully. Outside the reef, in a depth of around 15 metres, turn to your left, keeping the cliff on your left shoulder and soon you will note some large boulders. More gullies appear every few metres to invite you back into the reef. Some will end in caves and some lead you into other gullies, bringing you back outside the reef. One thing they all have in common is a richness of marine life. It was here, under the cliffs, that I stumbled across a lead cannon ball, a relic of the old French fort which protected the Scottish border from English invaders and which lent the point its name. You can still see a couple of its big guns on top of the cliffs above the site. If you continue finning around in this direction, you will eventually end up in Little Leeds Bay (dive site 83). This is a superb scenic dive and it is easy to while away an hour underwater in a very pleasant fashion.

In very poor weather, when a stiff westerly or northwesterly wind is blowing, Fort Point offers some protection from the elements and, because of its proximity to the harbour, you can still dive here if the skipper deems it safe. Do not fin through the gullies but explore the site behind the islet Luff Hard. It is mainly weed and there are a lot of pipefish and large scorpion fish to be seen. If you venture east, depth will be around 13 metres. There is a lot of debris, as this is the outer fairway to the harbour and junk has been dumped here over the years, so it makes for a good rummage dive. As you are in the fairway of a busy harbour, do ensure that you return to the Luff Hard area to surface. Only dive this site if you have excellent boat cover and a delayed surface marker buoy. This rummage dive is a worthwhile site in its own right but the dive around Fort Point is far superior.

Dive no. 85

Twisted boiler of the Mauretania

Name
Mauretania

Location
Wrecked on Buss Craig, the northernmost island of the group known as the Hurkers (dive site 86)
GPS coordinates N5552.75 W0205.15

Depth
16 metres

Conditions
Scenic wreckage and fantastic gullies, very tidal. Visibility 3–15 metres

Access
Boat only

Diver experience
Sports diver

Dive site
The *Mauretania* was wrecked on Buss Craig in 1927, twenty years after being launched from the Greenock shipyard. This wreck, of course, is not the grand ocean liner and Blue Riband-holder RMS *Mauretania*, just a small steam trawler with a big name. I am not even sure, in fact, if this is the correct spelling of this ship's name, as every piece of information gathered on this wreck uses a slightly different spelling. I would, however, think it a safe bet that this little boat used the same name as the massive

Cunard liner which was launched in the same year, perhaps hinting at the pride this little vessel's owners took in her. On a cold and foggy March day, the *Mauretania* tried to find her way into Eyemouth harbour. The group of rocks known collectively as the Hurkers (dive site 86) form a treacherous natural barrier that guards its mouth and the *Mauretania* ran straight onto the northernmost of these rocks, known as Buss Craig. There are some fantastic images of this boat perched totally high and dry on the rock, but it wasn't long before the North Sea claimed her. Her remains lie around the rock, mainly concentrated around the northwestern face of Buss Craig. The wreck has undergone many changes over the years, and there is likely to be more than one shipwreck here, as these rocks have claimed many victims. Checking through my logbook I find details of a wreck known as the *Mauretania* with a boiler, engine block and propeller, yet the wreck that I describe in this dive has neither propeller nor engine block. This suggests either another wreck in the area or that the propeller and engine have been salvaged. Taking into account the layout of the site, I am sure there is another wreck around the Hurkers. Even the wreck I describe here has changed in the last year or so, as she is slowly breaking up.

If you dive with Marine Quest, you will enter the water and fin down the steep slope of the rock. General depth will be around 12–14 metres and if you are lucky, visibility will exceed 10 metres. As you fin down, you will run along a length of pipe. This is the *Mauretania*'s funnel. Marine life covers the site and cheeky little Yarrel's blennies peek out from their holes in the reef. The seafloor is of coarse sand and shell, making this a bright site, and the surrounding peaks and gullies are smothered by swathes of orange-and-white dead man's fingers and plumose anemones. This is truly a very scenic spot and would be well worth diving even if there were no wreck here. On the sand there now lies a large structure. At first I could not tell which part of the ship I was looking at, but noted the spools of steel cable and was able to identify it as the trawl net winch. Flattened plates and pipes surround the site and anchors can be seen. A fully intact boiler used to rest here but just a year later, the forces of the North Sea had twisted it so that its internal pipe work looked like a corkscrew. A year after that, and the boiler had vanished, but its remains can still be seen. An obvious gully opens up on the wall to the west of the wreck site and there is a lot of wreckage gathered around its mouth. If it's a calm day and the tides are slack, fin up this gully. It will shallow but the marine life is amazing. Stunted plumose anemones cling to the rocks, fed by the strong tides that surge through here, but they are unable to grow tall because of the tides' ferocity. Gobies, shrimps and lobsters abound. Schools of small pollack and coalfish shimmer along the gully and larger specimens hang in the tide, reluctant to budge an inch as the diver fins by. This is spectacular scenic diving. Ballan wrasse are also common in the kelpy channels.

It is here, in around 8 metres of water, and where the gully takes a dog-leg bend to the south, that the remains of the boiler can be viewed. It has been wedged into a hole in the gully wall by the force of the seas that can surge angrily over these rocks.

This gully now becomes too shallow to explore much further and you will need to fin back to the dog-leg where a side gully breaks through to the outside of the rock. A sand-and-shell seafloor abuts the base of the anemone-encrusted walls. Edible crabs lie partially buried in the sand and razorshells lie discarded in large numbers. Now out in the open, away from the rock, it's likely that the tide will catch you, giving you little option but to go with the flow and send up your delayed surface marker buoy. This is one of the area's most spectacular scenic wreck dives and if the tide enables you to do so, don't miss exploring the spectacular gullies.

Sunstar at The Hurkers

Dive no. 86

Name
The Hurkers

Location
Large rocks, north of the entrance to Eyemouth harbour
GPS coordinates N5552.65
W0205.09

Depth
16–18 metres

Conditions
Very tidal islands.
Average visibility 8 metres

Access
Boat only

Diver experience
Sports diver/dive leader

Dive site
Buss Craig, with its wreck of the *Mauretania*, is described in dive site 85, and making up the group called the Hurkers are Hincar Rock, Briggs Rock and, the largest, Hurker Rock. These are the fang-like rocks that are clearly visible from the harbour mouth. Waves crash over them in bad conditions but in calm, sunny weather the Hurkers make a fantastic site for scenic diving. All the rocks can be dived in a single dive, although because of the number of gullies and the level of tidal movements, you are likely to need a number of dives to form a picture of the whole site. This is definitely a slack water dive. If you attempt to dive this site with the tide running, you will immediately lose the impressive walls and be blasted out to a flat reef covered by brittle stars, giving you a very mundane dive. Dropping into the water, depth will vary from

14–18 metres. Near-vertical walls fall onto flat bedrock, all of which is covered by dead man's fingers. The beauty of the Hurkers lies in the multiple vertical-sided gullies that cut through the islands. The kelp-covered walls fall straight from the surface to the seafloor. The seafloors inside the gullies are covered in coarse sand and shells and it is fantastic to fin through these beautiful gullies in sunlit conditions. There is always some water movement in the gullies, even near slack water or when only small neap tides are predicted, which makes finning hard work for the diver but which means that the marine life is stunning. Big schools of pollack and coalfish congregate in the gullies and the walls are covered in squat lobsters, nudibranchs and big edible crabs. Sunstars crawl along the seafloor and you have a very good chance of finding a wolffish hiding in a cave in the gully walls. This site may be right out from the harbour but don't let that put you off. If conditions are good, the tide is slack and you get the opportunity to dive this site, make sure you take the chance. You are likely to be rewarded with one of the best scenic dives the area can offer.

Squat lobster at Green Ends Gully

Dive no. 87

Name
Green Ends Gully

Location
On the southeast side of Eyemouth harbour, near Aquastars Dive Centre

Depth
13 metres

Conditions
Very nice, easy dive. Some tide at mouth of main gully. Average visibility 6 metres

Access
Shore dive. Aim to dive around high tide for easy access
Parking area £3 charge

Diver experience
Ocean diver

Dive site
Just beyond the southern ex-tremity of the St Abbs and

Eyemouth Voluntary Marine Reserve lies a little-known dive site that is regularly overlooked by the masses. In fact, I had to ask directions at Aquastars Dive Centre to find it, as it had been around ten years since I had last dived the site. In that time, Eyemouth harbour has been massively redeveloped and the old access to the site no longer exists. Thankfully, though, the dive site remains unchanged. There is a car park right at the head of the gully (£3 parking charge) and it's only a very short walk along a concrete path to the entry point. If it's a high tide you can almost get straight in, but if the tide is low, it can be a bit of a guddle. The effort is well worth it, though, as depth is quickly gained and the narrow confines of the kelpy access route are quickly left behind. Soon the depth becomes 8 metres within a sheer-sided gully around 5 metres wide. Pipefish are commonly found here in clumps of weed on the seafloor.

Around 20 metres along the gully, the depth starts to drop off again, and on the left-hand side a large flat slab of rock forms a massive overhang. It's full of cracks and crevices with larger recesses at its base. It may be the colours which strike you first. There are the usual dead man's fingers in orange and white, but the rocks themselves are covered in yellow, pink and orange sponges and encrusting growths which make the site very pretty. Take a closer look in this area and you will find Yarrel's blennies, scorpion fish, lobsters, squat lobsters and many different types of nudibranch. For macro-photographers it's delightful, with all that colourful negative space to fill. Opposite the overhang, a gully branches off at right angles from the right-hand side of the main gully. Depth shallows and small rounded boulders cover the seafloor. There is a nice archway on the right-hand side in here, if you want to take a look for it. Staying in the main gully and heading offshore from the overhang, you will pass through a narrow gap. There is a nice sandy-floored gully, 13 metres deep, to be found at the seaward end of the main gully. By following the wall round to the right, you will find a submerged reef rising around 5 metres off the seafloor. There is a little more tidal movement here so there is lots of life to see. Velvet-backed swimming crabs fill every crevice in this site, which has a reputation for octopus sightings too, although they have recently been infrequent. The coarse sand at the base of this gully is home to prawns, tiny flatfish and gobies that lie partially buried in the sand. The end of the gully is marked by a couple of large boulders, covered in soft corals including plumose anemones, confirming that the tide has a greater effect in this area. They also make a good feature to mark the end of the first dive at this site. Now the diver just needs to retrace their route back to the main gully, past the overhang and back to the exit point. Planning to arrive back here at high tide makes the exit a lot easier on the diver burdened with heavy kit. The dive successfully completed, the diver can plan to explore Green Ends Gully further on the next visit. A very rewarding dive from the shore that demands little effort if planned around high tide.

Dive no. 88

Name
Agate Point

Location
Offshore from golf clubhouse
GPS coordinates N5552.46
W0204.70

Depth
18 metres maximum

Conditions
Strong tidal movement can be experienced. Slack water recommended. Average visibility 8 metres

Access
Boat only

Diver experience
Sports diver

Dive site

Agate Point lobster

On shore, above the cliffs, the clubhouse of the golf course is just visible. In the gentle swell at the edge of the reef, a small outcrop of rock can occasionally be seen, marking the site of Agate Point. Here, underwater, a small archway is found, far smaller than the famous Cathedral Rock of St. Abbs (dive site 74) but extremely scenic nonetheless. Depth on the seaward side of the archway drops to over 20 metres, where a reef forms and rises up a metre or so out of the coarse sandy sea floor. The tide rips along here so slack water is preferable unless you want a nice drift dive. Entering the archway, which is around 14 metres deep, you will move from the outer reef through the wall into a gully running south, parallel to the outer wall. Depth in here is slightly shallower at around a maximum of 17 metres. You will find some shelter from the tide but you will only escape it fully at slack water. Because of all this water movement, marine life here is exceptional and orange-and-white dead man's fingers and plumose anemones cover the gully. Large boulders make up the sea floor. Underneath these, lobsters can commonly be seen. Octopus are here too but they are masters of camouflage, usually hiding in a crevice or nestled in the soft corals. The walls here are also adorned with soft corals and encrusting marine life, as you would expect from a high-energy site. Fish life is also excellent, with schools of pollack, vividly-coloured ballan wrasse, butterfish and, if you look closely, a lot of long-spined scorpion fish on the rocks. Nudibranchs also abound, so if you have a macro-kit on the camera, this is a prime site. This gully does eventually open up into a bay to the south, and here you will find the wreck of the *President*, described in dive site 89. If you have enough gas you can merge both dives together.

The President *wreck*

Name
President

Location
Wrecked in Gully at Whup Ness, 1 km south of Eyemouth harbour
GPS coordinates N5552.18 W0204.39

Depth
17 metres

Conditions
Easy wreck dive surrounded by colourful walls and gullies. Average visibility 8 metres

Access
Boat only

Diver experience
Ocean diver

Dive site
On 29 April 1928, in thick fog, the SS *President* ran aground and wedged herself stern-first into Whup Ness gully, just south of Agate Point (dive site 88). She became a total loss and broke up completely. Being partially perched on the shore, the wreck was well salvaged and no large propeller remains at this site. There is still a lot to see, though, and the remains of the *President* lie in a very scenic gully. I like to dive this wreck by being dropped off the boat to the south of the gully and from here you can fin onto the outer wall of the point. The walls are dramatic and fall down to 17 metres, covered in swathes of dead man's fingers. Caves and crevices open up at the base of the cliffs, filled with leopard-spotted gobies and squat lobsters. Fin along with the wall at your left shoulder and squeeze through the narrow gap between the tip of the point and an off-lying boulder. Rounding the point, you will notice that depth starts to shallow. You are now in the gully and will soon note rusty steel on the seafloor. Large mooring bollards, cogs and winches can all be seen, but the largest items are the *President*'s two boilers. Colourful ballan wrasse and cod hide in the boilers and smaller fish and shrimps inhabit the red kelp and weed which covers the top of them. Keep an eye out for octopus too. Continue inshore and the gully will narrow. Huge box sections of the *President* litter the floor here and the ends of large brass pipes stick out of the sand and weed. After around 30 metres, the gully becomes completely blocked and it's time to turn round and enjoy the deeper wreckage. On leaving the confines of this gully veer left, passing over more wreckage and the second boiler. After exploring this, if you have enough gas and the tide permits, you can fin on to the north and find yourself in some very nice gullies. If you are lucky you will find yourself in the gully that leads you to the archway at Agate Point as described in dive site 88. If you plan to do this, let your boat cover know in advance, as it is quite a distance and tidal flow can be strong once you leave the protection of the *President*'s gully. Pack a delayed surface marker buoy and enjoy yourself.

Dive no. 90

Name
Mike's Reef

Location
One mile directly off Eyemouth
harbour

Depth
16–25 metres

Conditions
Fantastic reef. Average visibility
10 metres

Access
Boat only

Diver experience
Sports diver/dive leader

Dive site
Alex Struthers, a buddy of mine,
had agreed to free a snagged
lobster pot for a local fisher-
man. I offered to help him and
we headed out in the Eyemouth
and District Sub Aqua Club's
boat *Aquanaut*. I am so glad we
did, as we experienced some
spectacular diving that day. On
finding the buoy which marked
the trapped pots, I took a transit
back onto the shore. The Eyemouth golf clubhouse was smack-

Diver in gully at Mike's Reef

bang in between the two biggest islands of the Hurkers that lie just off Eyemouth
Harbour. To find the site, head out on that transit for around one mile and when the
depth on the sounder reads 16 metres before dropping rapidly to 25 metres, you are
at the site. As far as I know, this site had never been dived before and has not been
since, which is a shame as it is amazing. Dropping down the shotline, the visibility was
excellent at 10 metres. We soon found the trapped pot and dealt with it, leaving us the
rest of the dive to explore the reef. We initially found ourselves on flat bedrock at 16
metres. Dead man's fingers absolutely carpeted this reef but it didn't look too exciting
otherwise, until, that is, I noted a gully cutting into the bedrock and dropping 5 metres

onto a coarse sandy seafloor. I dropped into the gully and finned offshore, startling a large cod that appeared to be dozing in the shelter of the gully. Beautiful dahlia- and deepwater-anemones lined the bottom of the wall. It was incredibly scenic. Finning further along the gully, it made a 90 degree turn and opened out onto a rocky slope, leading down to the seafloor in 25 metres. This site reminded me of the Anemone Gullies dive site at St Abbs (dive site 58). That site is held in high regard by many divers but here, off Eyemouth, is a similar one which nobody dives. I am going to make a point of getting out and diving this reef again and providing GPS coordinates. I recommend this dive to anyone wishing to try out a new site, although be aware that the shipping channel from the harbour will pass near here, so good boat cover is essential.

Dive no. 91

U-714C *screw and hydroplane*

Name
U-714C

Location
Off Eyemouth
GPS coordinates unavailable.
Contact Marine Quest to
arrange dive

Depth
51–58 metres

Conditions
Magnificent World War Two
Type-VIIC U-boat. Average
visibility 8 metres

Access
Boat only

Diver experience
Technical diver

Dive site
If you were to let an image form in your mind of a U-boat, the vessel that would appear would most likely be the Type VII. From bath toys we enjoyed as children to submarines in war films, the Type VII has often played in the starring role. It's the archetypal submarine and more Type VIIC U-boats were made than any other class of boat in the German navy. One completely intact Type VII U-boat is on display at a museum near Kiel in Germany, but we also have one in the Firth of Forth, although this intact Type VIIC lies 51–58 metres below the surface.

The Type VII U-boat was such a successful weapon that many variants were designed to specialise in mine-laying or as torpedo supply vessels. The class of vessel was identified by a letter after their type. The vessel in the Firth of Forth is C-class, denoting that this boat carried torpedoes. Named *U714C,* she was sunk in a depth charge attack by the frigate HMSAS *Natal* on 14 March 1945, just before the end of hostilities. She was armed with 14 torpedoes on a mission and had four bow torpedo tubes and one stern tube. This World War Two wreck is 66 metres long, large for a submarine of that era but still 34 metres shorter than the 100-metre long K-boats also found in the Firth of Forth (dives sites 30 and 31). This class of submarine also had a thicker steel hull than usual, to increase diving depth. The size of *U-714C* makes her ideal for a dive along the hull and back, taking into account the depth at which she is lying.

Dropping down the shotline, the diver will most likely stop at around 45 metres to attach a strobe to the line, to help relocate it at the end of the dive. The water here is usually clear but dark. The first thing the diver sees are the patches of orange-and-white plumose anemones that cover the wreck. Landing on the wreck near the stern, the diver will soon realise that the U-boat is listing around 40 degrees to starboard. On the deck at the stern the damage caused by the depth charges is visible on both the port and starboard side of the wreck, but it is otherwise incredibly intact. Finning forward at deck level, an open escape hatch is visible, while the deck hatch itself lies on the seafloor. It is said that the hatches were designed with hinges made from poorer quality steel, which have rotted away, leaving the surprisingly large hatch-cover to fall from its mount. All the deck hatches on this wreck now lie on the starboard side. There is also an angled torpedo loading hatch. Keep a look out for wolffish on the deck around here. Finning further forward, you will see that the deck becomes flat with a recess which once accommodated the machine-gun emplacement known as the 'winter garden', which was surrounded by railings and situated behind the conning tower. This has also now slipped from its mountings and fallen to lie in a broken mess on the seafloor on the starboard side of the wreck. This is where the anti-aircraft gun and 20-mm cannons will also be found, although I have not as yet noted them when exploring the wreck. Immediately forward of this is the most impressive conning tower, in position and completely intact, right down to the optics in the attack periscope. This can easily be viewed by moving to the top of the tower. There is another open hatch here, its cover also gone. In front of the conning tower can be seen the snorkel equipment and, on the starboard side of the conning tower, the radio direction finder (RDF) loop can be seen.

The diver can spend a lot of time investigating this area of the wreck, noting all the equipment that has fallen from the conning tower to lie on the seafloor. To get a picture of the whole wreck, fin forward, dropping down to the seafloor on the starboard side. There are gas cylinders here, most likely used for pumping ballast, and a canister full of inflatable yellow life jackets and life rafts. These were added to U-boats in the closing years of the war in light of heavy losses. Later boats, like *U-714C*, were also not fitted with a deck gun. Finning further forward, the starboard bow hydroplane lies in the mud but above this, the boat's anchor is located in its hawse. The bow itself is completely intact as if still slicing through the water, and the torpedo tubes can be viewed. Rising up onto the port side of the bow and heading aft, back to the stern, the diver will pass the much more visible port bow hydroplane. Drifting onto deck level and moving back to the stern, the diver soon passes the conning tower again. Time may be running short for exploring the submarine but there is one part of the wreck that must not be missed. At the stern, drop down once again to the seafloor where the starboard screw is visible. Finning under or around the stern, the twin rudders and stern hydroplanes can be clearly identified, even thickly coated as they are with plumose anemones. Then, emerging under the port side of the hull, the port screw can also be viewed, while between and above the screws, the stern torpedo tube can also be identified. You have now completed a tour of this magnificent U-boat and it is time to relocate the shotline, marked by the flashing strobe placed on the line earlier. Completing your long decompression stops, you will have time to reflect on a magnificent dive.

Dive no. 92

Topknot at the reef off Burnmouth Caves

Name
Reef off Burnmouth Caves

Location
Reef runs east offshore from middle cave
GPS coordinates N5551.93 W0204.30

Depth

18 metres

Conditions

Sandy gullies running between house-sized boulders. Average visibility 8 metres

Access

Boat only

Diver experience

Sports diver

Dive site

The reef off Burnmouth Caves is a fantastic dive site. The caves and this reef system can be completed in a single dive but I feel that by doing this you are experiencing only a part of this reef system. Both the caves and the reef can easily fill a whole dive in their own right and I now complete them as separate dives. Just at the southern end of the middle cave, there is a ridge of rock that comes to within 2 metres of the surface. This is known as Scout Cave. I asked Jim Easingwood to run over the site in his boat, *North Star*, and the ridge and the huge boulders appeared on the sounder, some rising a full 10 metres off the seafloor.

To find this reef, descend and fin offshore from the middle cave. Depth will soon increase from 10 metres to around 15 metres. The rock-and-kelp seafloor will be left behind as golden sand takes over. In front of you, you should now see the first of the house-sized boulders. They are basically rectangular in form, their surfaces covered with a dense coating of beautiful orange-and-white dead man's fingers. It is up to you where you go from here, as more of these huge anemone-encrusted boulders will be found as you travel offshore, with beautiful sandy avenues running between them. It truly is superb diving, and in a way similar to Conger Reef (dive site 82) which lies to the north, just off Weasel Loch (dive site 81). Marine life is spectacular here with schools of two-spot gobies swarming close to the walls and large flounders lying on the sand. Schools of small pollack and coalfish flirt along the walls. Larger solitary specimens lurk in the gullies or hang effortlessly in the tide at the more exposed areas. Edible crabs and lobster fill the cracks and crevices, along with squat lobsters and painted topshells. The clean golden sand and the walls of bright soft corals make this a magnificent site through which to fin, and visibility is usually around 10 metres. Rounding one of the boulders, the next one in line is found around 5 metres further offshore, once again surrounded by broad sandy gullies. General depths here are 18 metres but 22 metres can be reached.

Once you have explored the site and wish to ascend, there is a nice way to end the dive. If you fin to the south, you may pass through another fantastic sandy gully that ends in a dead end. It is blocked off by the reef that runs all the way out from the south wall of Scout Cave. Finning over the reef and heading back inshore, the water becomes shallower and you have a fantastic wall to fin along and explore as you ascend.

It is full of cracks and recesses and you will have an excellent chance of spotting a wolffish. Topknot, the flatfish which prefer to lie on rocky shelves rather than on sand, are commonly found in the wall recesses, often in pairs or groups of three. As the wall gets shallower, seaweeds and kelp start to take over and ballan wrasse become common sights. Lesser octopus are often seen here too. You will surface just off the caves. The reef off Burnmouth Caves is one of the most scenic sites in the area and finning along those broad, golden, sandy gullies is a fantastic experience. With clear sunny conditions this site is hard to beat.

Dive no. 93

Purple nudibranch

Name
Burnmouth Caves

Location
Large caves, 500 metres north of Burnmouth harbour
GPS coordinates N5551.93 W0204.30

Depth
15 metres maximum

Conditions
Excellent cave diving. Average visibility 8 metres

Access
Boat only

Diver experience
Sports diver

Dive site
Three large sea caves are to be found around 500 metres north of Burnmouth harbour. Working from south to north, they are called Horse Cave, Scout Cave and Dove Cave. Horse Cave and Scout Cave are glaringly obvious above the water to anybody passing by in a boat, as their gaping entrances face directly out to sea. Dove Cave is less visible, because it lies round the side of the point. This cave is of less interest to divers as it sits behind a drying reef, making it difficult to get to, and there is only around half a metre of water in it when you get there.

Horse Cave and Scout Cave do, though, make fantastic dives and each cave differs significantly from its neighbour. Horse Cave is the site I enjoy most here and it is a site not to be missed for the macro-photographer. While some divers whisk in, around and out of the cave in short order, taking the time really to look reveals some fantastic marine life. Falling off the back of the boat and descending in front of the southernmost cave, the diver descends to around 12 metres. Visibility is often in the range of 10 metres. Large kelp-covered boulders give way to a seafloor of smaller, smooth, rounded boulders as you fin into the cave mouth. Sea hares are found on the rocks here as well as smaller nudibranchs. I generally keep the north wall of the cave on my right shoulder as I fin in, passing over a large boulder as the entrance starts to form. The walls are vertical and reach right up above the surface at this point. They are fairly well covered by dead man's fingers, dahlia anemones, hydroids and sea urchins. In amongst all this life you will find butterfish, scorpion fish, velvet-backed swimming crabs and many different types of nudibranch in pink, blue, yellow and purple colorations. If you like hunting for sea slugs, then this is a prime spot. Finning further into the cave, the roof above you makes it a little darker and the walls gradually narrow in as you fin forward. The cave ends around 20 metres back from the entrance and it's time to turn round and fin back out. Take your time, though, as there are a lot of cracks and crevices in the walls to be investigated. I have found a few interesting fish here: two-spotted clingfish, Montagu's sea snail, tadpole fish and three-bearded rocklings, all of which are small and like to tuck themselves away in tiny holes in the wall. Finning out along the south wall of the cave, ambient light increases as you near the entrance and coverings of dead man's fingers become thicker. Even the odd patch of plumose anemones can be seen. There are some nice individual white specimens on top of larger rocks on the seafloor all the way into the cave. At the mouth of the cave you will remember the large boulder beside the north wall. It's a good idea to cross over the cave to that side now as you are making your way out of Horse Cave and into Scout Cave, which lies just to the north. All you need to do is follow the wall round, keeping it on your left shoulder, and a couple of minutes of finning will take you into the cave. This one is completely different; narrowing and becoming shallower once you enter it and cutting back much further into the headland. Once you are well inside, you may have only a metre of water above your head. You can surface and take a quick look at the weird brown rock formations on the roof of the cave, illuminated by your dive light. Divers will generally be in single file by this stage as the cave has narrowed so much. Once you have explored enough, make your way back to the entrance where, if you have enough gas, you can go on to explore part of the reef outside of the caves, but if you are an underwater photographer, it's likely that you will not have thought about leaving the first cave until gas reserves meant you had to.

Because these caves face directly out to sea, this site should be avoided if there is a surge or significant swell.

Dive no. 94

U-12 *conning tower surrounded by whiting*

Name
U-12

Location
14 miles out from Eyemouth
GPS coordinates unavailable. Contact Marine Quest to arrange dive

Depth
42–48 metres

Conditions
Wreck is covered in sections by netting. Deep air or trimix dive. Average visibility 8
metres

Access
By charter boat. Contact Marine Quest

Diver experience
Advanced diver/technical diver

Dive site
Eighteen miles out into the Firth of Forth from Eyemouth lies the recently-discovered wreck of a German submarine, identified as *U-12*. The wreck lies intact on a seafloor of mud at a depth of 48 metres. She makes a fantastic wreck dive, one of the best in the Forth.

U-12 is an historically important U-boat as she was the first submarine ever to carry an aircraft on her deck, to be deployed at sea. *U-12* was also the sister ship of *U-9* which, on 22 September 1914, under the command of Kapitänleutnant Otto Weddingen, sank three British light cruisers, HMS *Aboukir*, HMS *Hogue* and HMS *Cressy*, in less than 75 minutes. *U-9* became instantly famous. She survived the war but her sister ship *U-12* did not. When she had her own run-in with three British ships, the destroyers HMS *Ariel*, HMS *Acheron* and HMS *Attack*, it would be the British that would come out victorious.

The day before the battle, *U-12* was seen on the surface by a trawler. The sighting was eventually reported to the destroyers that were hunting her, along with the light cruiser HMS *Fearless*. *U-12* did not wait around to be found and carried on her deadly business, sending a steamship to the bottom in the outer Firth of Forth. The screen of destroyers which had been sweeping the east coast of Scotland moved towards her newly-reported position and saw the sub on the surface. *U-12* saw the destroyers coming and crash-dived to 25 metres, readying two of her four torpedo tubes for use. Kapitänleutnant Hans Kratzsch may have seen the opportunity to emulate Kapitänleutnant Weddingen, Germany's U-boat hero, by sinking his own three British warships. On this occasion, though, the destroyers were aware of the presence of a U-boat in the area. Kapitänleutnant Kratzsch gave the order to come to periscope depth. There was immediately an ear-splitting crash as the periscope was blown clean off the conning tower. *U-12* had come to periscope depth when HMS *Ariel* was almost on top of her. Seconds later, the bows of the ship rammed *U-12* on the port side, just forward of the conning tower. The sub rolled over 90 degrees and was forced under. Her ballast tanks were blown and when she surfaced, the destroyers shelled her. Ten men managed to escape the sub, while 19 of their comrades were not so lucky: the conning tower hatch had jammed and they became trapped. She now lies on the sea floor 48 metres down, a relic of a very famous class of submarine that makes a fantastic dive for a wreck diver.

Being the highest point on the wreck, the conning tower is usually the target for the shotline placement and is usually the first thing the diver sees on descending to the wreck. The conning tower is easily identifiable and on close inspection, you can make out its brass port holes and their wiper arms. Finning aft along the hull, skirting some old fishing net that has wrapped tightly into the wreck, the diver will note an open hatch. The pressure hull has rotted away, opening up holes and exposing pipes where marine life can hide. Schools of bib surround this wreck and there are some fairly large specimens. Big lobsters also like it here and they are a common sight. The hull soon tapers as the diver arrives at the stern and the distinctive twin torpedo tubes come into view. The door is missing from the port tube but it still houses a torpedo. A large lobster also lives here, unaware of its explosive surroundings. The starboard tube is empty, proof of the Kapitänleutnant's last-minute actions. As reported in the *New York Times*, he fired one of his torpedoes in a desperate attempt to strike his enemy a blow even though he was essentially blind, the periscope having been shot off by HMS *Ariel*. Directly below the stern tubes are the twin screws. They look quite small and I wonder how these little screws managed to power this boat so far. It's an impressive sight for the diver to be on the seafloor here, looking up at the screws and the torpedo tubes. Finning forward, the conning tower soon comes into view again. Taking time to examine this, the diver will note that the tower hatch is now off, possibly ripped away by a trawl net in the years since the trapped sailors desperately tried to free it and escape. Further forward and on the port side, the damage caused by HMS *Ariel* is clearly visible. On the deck near here can be seen a couple of interesting features: a pair of brass hydrophones, an early listening device. The forward hatch is also open and looking inside, the diver can catch a glimpse of a white toilet bowl still gleaming in the torchlight. At the most forward part of the main wreckage, the diver can clearly view the two bow torpedo tubes, their doors tightly closed. The bow itself has broken off and its wreckage lies apart from the main remains of *U-12*.

This wreck is not large and the diver can survey all of it in a single dive at a general maximum depth of 48 metres. Long decompression stops will mount up and so excellent gas management is required. Visibility at this site varies. On my dives I experienced best visibility of 10 metres, poor for a wreck this far offshore, and I expect the average visibility to be much better. Video taken of a dive on *U-12*, with visibility at well over 20 metres, has shown how good it can be.

There is an interesting story relating to one of the survivors of U-12. The pilot Volker managed to escape from his prisoner of war camp. He made his way to Hull where he gained employment as an able-bodied seaman on the Swedish bark *Ironstrop*. On 1 October 1915 *Ironstrop* was stopped and searched by *U-16*. This was excellent news for Volker who completed his escape by boarding the submarine. He was then assigned the role of war pilot on *U-44* but did not manage to see out the war. He lost his life when she was sunk on 12 August 1917.

Dive no. 95

Name
Ross Point

Location
Reef just south of Burnmouth harbour
GPS coordinates N5550.35 W0203.37

Depth
13 metres

Conditions
Shallow reef. Visibility around 10 metres can be expected

Access
Boat dive

Diver experience
Ocean diver

Dive site
The main interest at this site is the colony of grey seals which laze about on the reef top. If you enter the water, there is a good chance that one of them will visit you. They are in no way as bold as their cousins on the Farne Islands just over the border, but you can expect a few close passes. Apart from the seals, there is a lot of life to be found at this site. Dropping into the water

Grey seal at Ross Point

just off the reef, depth should be around 12 metres. The seafloor is tide-swept bedrock covered with a light dusting of coarse sand. It was here that I had my only encounter with a sole. The tide can run strongly here and it's best to head inshore where you will pick up some attractive gullies and see some amazing rock formations. These are easy to explore, are full of life and, best of all, they provide shelter from the tide. You can expect to find lobster, edible crabs and luminous orange-and-green Devonshire cup-corals. The gullies are covered in dead man's fingers and, their tops being shallow, are topped by long flowing throngs of kelp. A closer look at the walls reveals pipefish, sea urchins and nudibranchs. If you would like to have a seal encounter, Ross Point offers you a reasonable chance of success. If, however, these furry friends do not wish to play, you will not be disappointed with the gullies and the smaller marine life that makes them its home.

Marine Quest dive boat Jacob George

Dive no. 96

Name
Brisset Rock

Location
Just south of Burnmouth harbour, 200 metres off Ross Point (dive site 95)
GPS coordinates N5550.35 W0203.37

Depth
19 metres

Conditions
Superb wall dive around island. Average visibility 8 metres

Access
Boat only

Diver experience
Sports diver/dive leader

Dive site

I first dived Brisset Rock by accident. I initially thought I would drop in for a snorkel with the three or four grey seals that were dozing on top of the rock. The tide was so swift, though, that snorkelling was impossible so I donned my scuba gear. I am so glad I did, as this is one of the more magnificent dive sites found near Burnmouth. On descending, it becomes apparent that Brisset Rock, rather than being an isolated island, forms part of a chain of rocky outcrops. Brisset Rock is the only one of these peaks to break the surface, although even it is covered at high tide. On descending at the southern end of the rock, you immediately have to make a choice between finning round either the inshore or the offshore side of the rock. You are choosing between two completely different experiences, as the two sides of the rock are quite unlike each other. The inshore side of the rock is shallower, the average depth being around 14 metres. Marine life is spectacular and the wall is covered in orange-and-white dead man's fingers from the bottom right up to the kelp fronds at the top. Coarse sand

and boulders make up the seafloor. It is truly spectacular, shallow, scenic wall diving. By contrast, the offshore side is deeper at around 18 metres. The walls are no longer vertical but still very steep. Only patches of dead man's fingers sporadically decorate these outer walls. Sea urchins are more prolific and large dahlia anemones are common. If you initially decide to opt for the deeper side of the island, it pays to fin along the bottom of the cliff. As the wall is devoid of cover, the marine life gathers in the fissures, cracks and crevices that run up and along the wall here. You will find that there is still plenty of life on this side but you have to look a little harder to find it. The red eyes of the ever-more-common velvet-backed swimming crab peek out of the cracks, claws and pincers at the ready as this aggressive little creature adopts an angry pose. Many of its larger cousins are here too, edible crabs slotting into cracks that seem to have been designer-made for them. Larger boulders are found at the base of the cliff and it is worthwhile looking under these, as cod and ling are often present. Sometimes a huge lobster sits in a recess surrounded by a brood of its hatched fry. Spider crabs sit on top of the boulders and, looking closely, the fantastic Devonshire cup-corals can be viewed. Once you are close enough to look at small creatures like that, you will soon start to notice pipefish, gobies and nudibranchs. While on first impressions, then, this outer side of the island looks fairly barren, it certainly turns out to be anything but. This wall continues for around 100 metres before the end of the island is reached. There is then an area of sand before the next section of reef starts to rise out of the seafloor. It is here that you have the chance to dart back into the shoreward side of the rock and enjoy the scenic side of the island. Passing over the sandy area can be a rewarding experience. I noted flashes of silver that turned out to be a ball of sand eels darting in and out of the sand which had attracted a gang of pollack. These sat motionless just off the sand before flashing at high speed into the sand eels and returning to their stationary position to digest their meal. You cannot afford to blink. Finning round the island, the walls become vertical and soft corals cover every piece of rock and looking directly up, seals can be seen on the surface, swimming over to rest on dry land.

Brisset Rock is a fantastic and completely under-dived site. No matter which side of the rock you decide to explore, you will have a fantastic dive. This underwater reef runs along the seafloor to East and West Hurker, 500 metres to the north. The diving around these rocks is shallow and kelpy and is therefore less spectacular.

On the day at Brisset Rock when I tried to dive with seals, I caught only a brief glimpse of them in the distance. Until, that is, I surfaced and was returning to the boat. I looked down and saw two large grey shapes heading towards me at high speed. Two seals had decided to frighten the living daylights out of me, veering away at the last second. My imagination helped, of course. I had only the week before watched reports of the vertical attacks being performed by great white sharks at seal colonies in South Africa. Don't worry, though: the only shark seen here was a 3-metre basking shark which made a few appearances around this site in 2008.

Dive no. 97

Diver next to the boiler of the East Neuk

Name
East Neuk

Location
Near Burnmouth harbour
GPS coordinates N5550.47
W0203.16

Depth
23 metres

Conditions
Small wreck dive, covered in
marine life. Average visibility 8
metres

Access
Boat only

Diver experience
Sports diver

Dive site

This wreck is known as the *East Neuk* although there is some debate as to whether it
has been misidentified. The wreck was found around 7 years ago and after some failed
attempts, I eventually managed to dive it and have had some great dives since. The
wreck is well broken-up but there are still lots of interesting sections to see. On a clear
day, the wreck is a very scenic sight. Light bounces off the seafloor of coarse sand and
divers will experience a bright dive. Descending down the shotline, the first thing the
diver may see is the fairly large propeller. Only two of the blades are now visible and
their tips are covered in dead man's fingers. Two anchors can also be viewed, just to
the starboard side of the prop. The prop is still connected to the prop shaft and this
leads you forward to a large engine block. You can still make out all the crank shafts,
even underneath their covering of barnacles and soft corals. Fish like to lie inside the
protected recesses of the engine block so take the time to have a good look and you
may see bib, ling, cod and conger eels as well as the more common ballan wrasse and
pollack. Moving forward again a short distance, a single large boiler rises around 4
metres off the seafloor. There are two furnaces where stokers once shovelled tons of
coal into the boilers but which now may be inhabited by the odd lobster. The smaller
boiler tubes above them are, however, full of life. Take a close look at these and you
will make some great finds. Juvenile lobsters squeeze themselves into the small pipes
for protection, Yarrel's blennies may look out at you from the safety of their pipes and

small edible crabs and prawns fill some of the other holes. While photographing some of these creatures I noted that shoals of small two-spot gobies tend to school in this area and I have seen them here on a number of occasions. There is a lot of marine life to encounter around the boiler, which is easily the largest remaining structure of the shipwreck. Its sides have deteriorated somewhat, exposing the internal pipes to the diver. Ballan wrasse like to live inside the boiler so have a look inside and see if you can catch a glimpse of them. Forward from here, the wreck peters out and only a large winch is found off the starboard side. The wreck is small and forms an oasis of life in an otherwise fairly uninspiring reef. On your way back to the shotline, make sure you have a quick look under the prop shaft, as last time I dived here there was a nice octopus sitting there. The *East Neuk* is a nice scenic wreck and a great way to let the novice diver experience their first wreck dive.

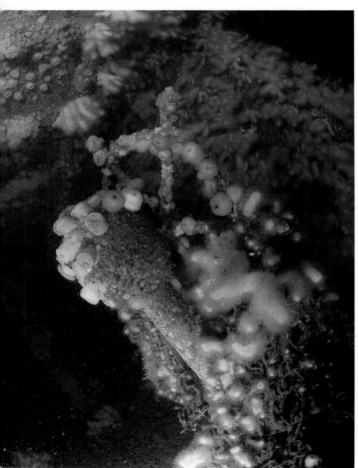

Exmouth *wreck auxiliary steering wheel*

Dive no. 98

Name
SS E*xmouth*

Location
Over 30 miles offshore from Eyemouth
GPS coordinates unavailable. Contact Marine Quest to arrange dive

Depth
38–58 metres

Conditions
Superb intact wreck dive. Deep air or trimix diving. Average visibility 15 metres

Access
Boat only, via Marine Quest

Diver experience
Advanced diver/technical diver

Dive site
With this wreck site over 30 miles out into the North Sea, Marine Quest's current charter boat *Silver Sky* takes up to three

hours to reach it from Eyemouth. There is plenty of time to ponder the sketches made by Stevie Adams, one of the very few divers ever to have reached and dived this site. This wreck was only located in late 2008 and at the time of writing, only two trips have succeeded in diving it. I was lucky enough to be on the second of those trips and can testify that the *Exmouth* is the best wreck in the area and the most sought-after by divers.

The *Exmouth* was a massive American cargo vessel, 100 metres long and weighing 4800 tonnes. Much like the mass-produced armed freighters known as 'liberty ships', 20-mm machine guns were mounted in circular turrets along the superstructure, with larger calibre guns found at the bow and stern. On 31 July 1944, *Exmouth* was sailing up the Firth of Forth, in ballast and travelling from Southend to Methyl when she ran into the eastern defensive minefield that protected the Firth of Forth. Why she did so is a mystery. She struck a British mine and sank shortly afterwards. No lives were lost.

Exmouth now lies in 53 metres of water and there is even a scour to 58 metres at the bow and stern. You don't need to go that deep, though, and I never went past the 50-metre mark. Soon, the dark shadow of this massive wreck will appear in the green water. Visibility at this site was 40 metres when first dived although only 10 metres on the second trip. The wreck lies listing to her starboard side and the shallowest point is the port side of the bridge, which lies around 38 metres deep. Here you will note a large circular structure. This is one of the gun turrets. It is so heavily encrusted in dead man's fingers that it will take a second or two to identify what you are looking at. Dropping down to the deck, aft of the bridge, and finning along the shallower side of two large holds, the aft superstructure and the sterncastle eventually come into view, a large gun is mounted upon the sterncastle. Finning through the sterncastle itself at deck level, you will note the alternate steering wheel in pristine condition, protected by its covering of soft corals. Taking the starboard companionway back out of the stern castle, you will pass a fire hose reel before re-emerging into the green ambient light. Derrick cranes lie tumbled across the rear holds. These have to be passed again before arriving back at the rear of the bridge. At 48 metres on the deeper side of the bridge, there is so much to see: another tower with its circular turret and 20-mm cannons, this one tilting over parallel to the seafloor as its tower has bent under the strain of the turret's weight.

Finning forward around the bridge you will see one of the most amazing sights that a diver can see. On the deck below you is the brass compass binnacle lying on its side. its green coloration immediately identifying an important feature of the bridge of this vessel. Beside this is a telegraph, although this was made of steel. Further forward a massive brass porthole lies on the deck. It's all there for the diver to look at, and will be for a long time to come, I hope, thanks to Marine Quest's policy of 'look- but-don't-touch' diving. The bell has not been found and is presumably still on the deck around the bridge area. Rising up the front of the bridge you may be lucky enough to note some black-and-white tiles. Looking closely, you will be able to make out the remains of a shower unit. The pipework and shower-head now lie across the deck. Further back into the wreckage gleams the white of a toilet bowl and a sink, presumably in what was the captain's quarters. My dive was over. I would have been more than happy to explore further but my bottom time of 28 minutes was up and I drifted up back to the shotline. This is an extremely large, intact shipwreck and is impossible to survey completely in one dive, unless you can use a sea scooter. My exploration did not include the bow section so I cannot at present comment on that section of this amazing wreck. Needless to say, that is one of the dives I intend to enjoy at the next possible opportunity.

This is a beautiful wreck, completely intact and lying in a depth that is suitable for deep air diving or a light trimix mix. Protected by 30 miles of the North Sea, the *Exmouth* still displays all her artefacts. You know you will have been extremely fortunate if you get the chance to dive the *Exmouth* as it is at present the most exciting shipwreck in the area. Opportunities to dive this wreck are few and far between but should never be missed.

Dive no. 99

Deep water Arctic anemone at Clipper Reef

Name
Clipper Reef

Location
South from Burnmouth
GPS coordinates N5549.86
W0200.28

Depth
36–43 metres

Conditions
Large boulders. Average
visibility 8 metres

Access
Boat only

Diver experience
Advanced diver

Dive site
The name of this dive site suggests a shipwreck, which is what we expected to find when we motored out to dive the site. The sounder suggested a ship-shaped obstruction rising 7 metres off the seafloor. That, sadly, was as close to a shipwreck as we got.

Diving down the shotline, piles of massive boulders came into view, so large that they were unlikely to be the ballast stones of an old sailing ship. It is said that this rock formation was caused by a natural event and it is the only disturbance on an otherwise flat seafloor. After dealing with the initial disappointment of there being no wreck at the site, we surveyed the rocks and found lots of long-clawed squat lobsters living between them. Large dahlia anemones and arctic anemones were also found. The water was dark but the visibility was good at 8 metres, although unfortunately only the odd fish darted around the reef. At such a depth, time passes very quickly and for a photographer the depth and darkness made this scenic site fairly unproductive. It would have been fantastic to find a shipwreck here but that is the chance you take when looking for new wrecks: sometimes you win and sometimes you get just a reasonable scenic dive. This is an interesting dive but not one I would rush back to complete again, especially when there are still undived sites to be explored out of Eyemouth.

Dive no. 100

Big winch on the Shadwan

Name
Shadwan

Location
2 miles north of Holy Island

GPS coordinates N5543.21 W0151.20

Depth
19 metres

Conditions
Broken-up wreck. Average visibility 8 metres

Access
Boat only

Diver experience
Sports diver

Dive site
The *Shadwan* is actually lying in English waters and I would have to venture back to the Middle Ages if I wanted to class this area as part of Scotland. I am therefore using creative licence to include her in this book of the wrecks and reefs of southeast Scotland, and excuse myself on the grounds that the *Shadwan* is regularly visited by the Eyemouth-based dive boats of Marine Quest. The *Shadwan* was built in 1877 and was a 1500-ton steamship. In her 11 years, she sailed round many of the ports of Europe and her final journey was from Yugoslavia to Leith in the Firth of Forth. Before she could make that safe harbour, though, force ten gales ripped out of the northeast and the *Shadwan* foundered with the loss of all her crew, two miles north of Holy island. The *Shadwan* is a very scenic but broken-up shipwreck and I find her flattened remains somewhat confusing to fin around. Mooring bollards and a couple of large winches are to be found a short distance away from the main part of the wreck. A spare propeller is also visible. It is completely surrounded by broken plates and box sections of the wreck. In the next section along, the boiler can be viewed but this feature is more than half- buried in the seafloor. This is a very pleasant dive when the conditions are good. The seafloor is just over 18 metres deep and comprises coarse gravel and pebbles. The visibility can often be very good. In the summer months the wreckage becomes a haven for pollack and whiting which school around the rusty steel. The tops of the winches and higher-standing parts of the wreckage also have a very slight covering of dead man's fingers. The *Shadwan* therefore does have some very nice features to explore and while her remains may not make for the most exciting of dives, the marine life and the good conditions that are often encountered at this site provide a very scenic swim around the remains of this old wreck.

Dive Centres

NAME	**THE DIVE BUNKER** Contact: Mark Blyth
ADDRESS	Lammerlaws Road, Burntisland, Fife, KY3 9BS
PHONE	01592 874380
E-MAIL	hamishdivedog@hotmail.com
WEB	*www.divebunker.co.uk*
SERVICES AVAILABLE	
GAS	Air, nitrox
BOAT	Yes, licensed for 12 divers
EQUIPMENT SALES	Yes, shop
EQUIPMENT SERVICING	Yes
TRAINING SCHOOL	5* PADI school
ACCOMMODATION	No

Edinburgh & Lothians

NAME	*EDINBURGH DIVING CENTRE* Contact: Dougy McEwan
ADDRESS	1 Watson Crescent, Edinburgh, EH11 1HD
PHONE	Phone: 0131-229-4838 Fax: 0131-622-7099
E-MAIL	sales@edinburghdiving.co.uk
WEB	
SERVICES AVAILABLE	
GAS	Air, Nitrox and Trimix
BOAT	No
EQUIPMENT SALES	Yes, large shop
EQUIPMENT SERVICING	Yes, Idest centre
TRAINING SCHOOL	Yes
ACCOMMODATION	No

NAME	**GM DIVING**
	Contact: Gordon Mackay
ADDRESS	22b Coates Gardens, Edinburgh, EH12 5LE
PHONE	07801 258943
E-MAIL	mail@gmdiving.com
WEB	www.gmdiving.com
SERVICES AVAILABLE	
GAS	No
BOAT	No
EQUIPMENT SALES	No
GUIDED DIVES	Yes
TRAINING SCHOOL	Yes
ACCOMMODATION	No

NAME	**MIKE CLARK UNDERWATER PHOTOS**
	Contact: Mike Clark
ADDRESS	24 Stoneyhill Drive, Musselburgh, Midlothian, EH21 6SQ
PHONE	Mobile: 07722 887278
E-MAIL	mikeclark100@talktalk.net
WEB	www.underwater-photos.co.uk
SERVICES AVAILABLE	
UNDERWATER PORTRAITS	Yes
GUIDED PHOTO DIVES	Yes
PRINT SALES	Yes
PHOTOGRAPHY COURSES	Yes

NAME	**TT DIVING**
	Contact: Stevie Gibson
ADDRESS	7 Waverley Crescent, Bonnyrigg
PHONE	Mobile: 07745 276562
E-MAIL	ttdiving@aol.com
WEB	
SERVICES AVAILABLE	
GAS	Air
BOAT	No
EQUIPMENT SALES	Yes, small Shop
EQUIPMENT SERVICING	Yes
TRAINING SCHOOL	Yes
ACCOMMODATION	No

NORTH BERWICK

NAME	AQUATREK
	Contact: Cam Small
ADDRESS	
PHONE	Mobile: 07790 929656
E-MAIL	info@aquatrek.co.uk
WEB	www.aquatrek.co.uk
SERVICES AVAILABLE	
GAS	Air, compressor at harbour
BOAT	Yes, *Thistle B*. Licensed for 12 divers
EQUIPMENT SALES	No
EQUIPMENT SERVICING	No
TRAINING SCHOOL	No
ACCOMMODATION	No

NAME	FORTH DIVING SERVICES
	Contact: Gary or Brian
ADDRESS	Forth Diving Services, Unit 6, Millwalk Business Park, North Berwick, EH39 5NB
PHONE	The shop number is 01620 890022 and Gary can be contacted out of hours on 07974 168606. The shop has varying opening hours and it is advisable to phone before visiting to ensure that it is open
E-MAIL	info@divesafariscotland.com
WEB	Shop www.divesafariscotland.co.uk
	Boat www.forthdivingservices.co.uk
SERVICES AVAILABLE	
GAS	Air, Nitrox, Trimix
BOAT	Yes, based at Dunbar. Licensed for 12 divers
EQUIPMENT SALES	Yes
EQUIPMENT SERVICING	Yes
TRAINING SCHOOL	5* PADI Instructor Development Centre
ACCOMMODATION	No

ST ABBS

NAME	DIVESTAY Contact: Billy & Alison Aitchison
ADDRESS	Westhaven, Brierylaw, St Abbs, TD14 5PH
PHONE	Telephone: 01890 771288 Mobile: 07802 330036
E-MAIL	enquiries@divestay.co.uk
WEB	www.divestay.co.uk
SERVICES AVAILABLE	
GAS	No
BOAT	Yes, Wavedancer 2. Licensed for 12
EQUIPMENT SALES	No
EQUIPMENT SERVICING	No
TRAINING SCHOOL	No
ACCOMMODATION	Yes, accommodates 12 people in two double and four twin bedrooms. Each spacious room has original shuttered windows, TV, radio, and wireless Internet, and plenty of room to relax in comfort

NAME	*LAZY G DIVER* DIVE BOAT Contact: Paul and Dawn O'Callaghan
ADDRESS	Priory View, Eyemouth Road, Coldingham, Berwickshire, TD14 5NH
PHONE	Phone: 018907 71525 Mobile: 0777 644 7183
E-MAIL	(Accommodation) prioryview@btinternet.com (Dive boat) paul@stabbsdiving.com
WEB	(Accommodation) www.prioryview.com (Dive boat) www.stabbsdiving.com
SERVICES AVAILABLE	
GAS	No
BOAT	Yes, *Lazy G Diver*, licensed for 12
EQUIPMENT SALES	No
EQUIPMENT SERVICING	No
TRAINING SCHOOL	No
ACCOMMODATION	Yes, Priory View. Can normally take 12 people in bed and breakfast accommodation. All rooms are *en suite* and have a digital TV, hospitality trays and hairdryer.

NAME	RACHEL AND PAUL CROWE
ADDRESS	Rock House, St Abbs, Berwickshire, TD14 5PW
PHONE	Paul (mobile): 07710-961-050
	Rachel: 01890-771945
E-MAIL	dementeddogfish@aol.com
WEB	www.divestabbs.com
SERVICES AVAILABLE	
GAS	Air
BOAT	Yes, *Tiger Lilly*, dive charter boat licensed for 12 divers
EQUIPMENT SALES	No
EQUIPMENT SERVICING	No
TRAINING SCHOOL	No
ACCOMMODATION	Yes, bunkhouse (sleeps 10), cottage (5) and bed and breakfast (3). Drying room. Breakfasts available. Can cater for large and small groups

NAME	SCOUTSCROFT HOLIDAY AND DIVING CENTRE
	Contact: Amanda
ADDRESS	St Abbs Road, Coldingham, Eyemouth, Berwickshire, TD14 5NB
PHONE	General enquiries: 01890 771338
	Diving enquiries: 01890 771669
E-MAIL	holidays@scoutscroft.co.uk or
	divescoutscroft@yahoo.co.uk
WEB	www.scoutscroft.co.uk
SERVICES AVAILABLE	
GAS	Yes, Air, Nitrox
BOAT	No
EQUIPMENT SALES	Yes, shop
EQUIPMENT SERVICING	Yes, suit repairs, regulator servicing and cylinder testing
TRAINING SCHOOL	No
ACCOMMODATION	Yes, caravan, self catering, bed and breakfast and half-board accommodation. Facilities include restaurant, lounge bar, function room, snooker lounge, Wifi, take-away and launderette

NAME	*SELKIE DIVE BOAT*
	Contact: Peter Gibson
ADDRESS	The Rest, Murrayfield, St Abbs, Berwickshire, TD14 5PP
PHONE	**Telephone:** 018907 71681
	Mobile: 07702 687606
	Fax: 018907 71312
E-MAIL	PeterGibson@stabbs.com (best contacted by phone)
WEB	n/a
SERVICES AVAILABLE	
GAS	No
BOAT	Yes, *Selkie*. Licensed for 12 divers
EQUIPMENT SALES	No
EQUIPMENT SERVICING	No
TRAINING SCHOOL	No
ACCOMMODATION	No

NAME	ST ABBS & EYEMOUTH VOLUNTARY MARINE RESRERVE RANGER SERVICE
ADDRESS	St Abbs & Eyemouth Voluntary Marine Resrerve (VMR), Rangers' Office, Northfield, St Abbs, Berwickshire, TD14 5QF
PHONE	Tel: 018907 71443
E-MAIL	Via website
WEB	www.marine-reserve.co.uk/volunteers-conservation/contact/contact.php
SERVICES AVAILABLE	
GAS	
BOAT	
EQUIPMENT SALES	
EQUIPMENT SERVICING	
TRAINING SCHOOL	
ACCOMMODATION	

EYEMOUTH

NAME	AQUAMARINE CHARTERS
	Contact: Derek Anderson
ADDRESS	Unavailable
PHONE	Tel: 01890 750481
	Mobile: 07860 804316
E-MAIL	Via website
WEB	www.aquamarine-charters.co.uk
SERVICES AVAILABLE	
GAS	No
BOAT	*Scimitar*
EQUIPMENT SALES	No
EQUIPMENT SERVICING	No
TRAINING SCHOOL	No
ACCOMMODATION	No

NAME	AQUASTARS DIVE CENTRE
	Contact: Jacqui or Peter
ADDRESS	Guns Green Basin, Eyemouth, Berwickshire, TD14 5SD
PHONE	Tel: 018907 50904
	Mobile: 07803 616201
	Fax: 018907 51470
E-MAIL	info@aquastars.co.uk
WEB	www.aquastars.co.uk
SERVICES AVAILABLE	
GAS	Air, Nitrox
BOAT	RIB charter
EQUIPMENT SALES	Yes, dive shop
EQUIPMENT SERVICING	Yes, equipment hire, cylinder testing, equipment repair, equipment servicing
TRAINING SCHOOL	PADI Scuba Diving Training School
ACCOMMODATION	No

NAME	**MARINE QUEST BOAT CHARTER** Contact: Jim and Iain Easingwood
ADDRESS	Harbourside, 33 Harbour Road, Eyemouth, Berwickshire, TD14 5HY
PHONE	Tel: 01890 752444 Mobile: 07780 823884
E-MAIL	info@marinequest.co.uk
WEB	www.marinequest.co.uk
SERVICES AVAILABLE	
GAS	Yes, Air, Nitrox and Trimix
BOAT	Two boats, *North Star* and *Silver Sky* and a third soon to be in service. All licensed for 12 divers each.
EQUIPMENT SALES	No
EQUIPMENT SERVICING	No
TRAINING SCHOOL	No
ACCOMMODATION	Yes, the newly-appointed Harbourside offers diver-friendly bed and breakfast accommodation. Non-divers also welcome.

Sources and further reading

Baird, Bob. 2009. *Shipwrecks of the Forth and Tay*. Whittles Publishing

Bennett, Geoffrey. 1999. *The Battle of Jutland*. Wordsworth Military Library

Campbell, John. 1986. *Jutland: An analysis of the fighting*. Conway Maritime Press

Ridley, Gordon. 1998. *Dive Scotland:* Volume III. Underwater World Publications

Warman, Carol. *A guide to diving in the St. Abbs and Eyemouth Voluntary Marine Reserve*. Cornwall Litho

Wood, Lawson. 1998. *Dive St. Abbs and Eyemouth*. Underwater World Publications

http://uncyclopedia.wikia.com

http/wapedia.mobi/en

www.chriscunard.com

www.german-navy.de

www.secretscotland.org.uk

www.worldwar1.co.uk